THE POEMS

OF

CHARLES FENNO HOFFMAN.

THE

POEMS

OF

CHARLES FENNO HOFFMAN.

COLLECTED AND EDITED

BY HIS NEPHEW,

EDWARD FENNO HOFFMAN.

PHILADELPHIA:
PORTER & COATES.
1873.

WESTCOTT & THOMSON,
Stereotypers and Electrotypers, Philada.

SHERMAN & CO.,
Printers, Philada.

PREFACE.

Charles Fenno Hoffman was born in New York in 1806. He entered Columbia College when fifteen years old, and remained there till the junior year, when he commenced the study of law in Albany. He was of too active a temperament for so quiet a life, and a number of his poems which appeared in the "Albany Gazette"* having met with a favorable reception, he gradually drifted away from his profession, and engaged in an occupation more congenial to his tastes. During his literary career, he was for a number of years a contributor to the "New York American," and afterward became editor of the "Knickerbocker Magazine" and the "Literary World." In October, 1833, starting from New York on horseback, he made a tour in the dead of winter

* Several of these poems may be found in this volume under the head of "Forest Musings."

through the North-western States to the Mississippi, and home through the South-west, Kentucky and Virginia. During nearly the whole of this adventurous ride he was entirely alone, with the exception of such chance companions as he would pick up on the way; and considering the intensity of the cold, the severity of the snow-storms and the unsettled state of the country, it is remarkable that he accomplished it without an accident. On his return to New York the following May he published an account of his trip in a series of letters entitled "A Winter in the West." He is also the author of "Wild Scenes in Forest and Prairie," "Grayslaer, a Romance," "The Life of Jacob Leisler" and numerous essays which have never been collected.

For the last twenty-five years, on account of ill-health, he has been obliged to forego all literary pursuits, and since his retirement, his writings have been for many years out of print, and his reputation has only been kept alive by "Monterey," "Sparkling and Bright," "Rosalie Clare" and other of his most popular songs which have found their way into the various compendiums of American literature. In placing this volume of his poems before the public I have been influenced solely by a feeling that on account of their literary merits they should be collected, and that the author would prefer this task be performed by some near relative whose affection for him entitled to assume so delicate an office. Conscious that I possess this qualification, I have been encouraged to undertake what has been to me a most agreeable labor. A complete edition of his poems would be impossible, as many of them appeared anonymously; but in the present volume I have included a number of pieces not contained in either of the previous editions. It is rather a venture to reproduce poems which have remained so long a time in obscurity; but in the conviction that a true appreciation of the beauties of nature and purity of sentiment are qualities which will always be admired, I have strong hopes that they will regain their former position of popularity with the public.

My uncle was a lover of nature and the natural. Most of his leisure was spent in excursions on the Hudson and into the Adirondacks, at that time a trackless wilderness. He was passionately fond of these wild haunts, and took a particular interest in the hunters and Indians, at that time the only inhabitants. He always enjoyed the greatest health and strength, and when on his rambles was perfectly indifferent to the weather or the accommodations he was obliged to put up with. Like all strong, simple-hearted men, love of country was one of his predominating characteristics. He took a special interest in our early traditions and made them the subjects of most of his prose writings. The motto of a writer in the West is emblematic of his life:

> Where can I journey to your secret springs,
> Eternal nature? Onward still I press,
> Follow thy windings still, yet sigh for more.
>
> GOETHE.

The following tribute to his character and authorship from his friend and cotemporary, Mr. Bryant, to whom I return my sincere thanks for his interest, has given me great encouragement in my work.

E. F. H.

CUMMINGTON, MASS., Aug. 5, 1873.

MY DEAR SIR:—I congratulate you on the completion of the task which you have undertaken of collecting the poetical productions of your uncle,

Charles Fenno Hoffman, whom, while he lived in New York, I was proud to reckon among my friends, and whose kindly and generous temper and genial manners won the attachment of all who knew him. His poems bear the impress of his noble character. They are the thoughts of a man of eminent poetic sensibilities, who delights to sing of whatever moves the human heart—the domestic affections, patriotic reminiscences, the traditions of ancient loves and wars, and the ties of nature and friendship. These thoughts are expressed in musical versification with the embellishments of a ready fancy. The friends of your uncle have reason to thank you for presenting them in this manner the moral and intellectual image of him whom they have had such reason to esteem.

I am, sir,

Very truly yours,

W. C. BRYANT.

E. FENNO HOFFMAN, ESQ.

CONTENTS.

FOREST MUSINGS.

LAYS OF THE HUDSON.

LOVE POEMS.

SONGS AND OCCASIONAL POEMS.

FOREST MUSINGS.

INSCRIPTION.

THE fragile bark whereon the Indian traces
  Rude tokens of his path for other eyes,
Sometimes outlasts the tree on which he places
    Anew the birchen scroll he thence had peeled,
  And while he wanders forth to other skies,
    Some curious Settler, ere his axe he wield,
The frail memorial careful bears away :—
So I have freely traced a woodland lay,
  In lines as quaint as chart of forest child,
Content, like him, if passing on my way,
  I cheer some friendly heart in life's dull wild—
A birchen scroll from birchen tree y'cleft,
A trail of moccasin in wildering forest left.

Forest Musings.

The Hunt is Up.

A MEDITATION.

THE hunt is up—
The merry woodland shout,
That rung these echoing glades about
An hour agone,
Hath swept beyond the eastern hills,
Where, pale and lone,
The moon her mystic circle fills;
Awhile across her slowly reddening disk
The dusky larch,
As if to pierce the blue o'erhanging arch,
Lifts its tall obelisk.

And now from thicket dark,
And now from mist-wreathed river
The fire-fly's spark
Will fitful quiver,
And bubbles round the lily's cup
From lurking trout come coursing up,

Where stoops the wading fawn to drink:
  While scared by step so near,
Uprising from the sedgy brink
The clanging bittern's cry will sink
  Upon the hunter's ear;
Who, startled from his early sleep,
  Lists for some sound approaching nigher—
Half-dreaming, lists—then turns to heap
  Another fagot on his fire,
And then again, in dreams renewed,
Pursues his quarry through the wood.

And thus upon my dreaming youth,
  When boyhood's gambols pleased no more,
And young Romance, in guise of Truth,
  Usurped the heart all theirs before;
    Thus broke Ambition's trumpet-note
      On visions wild,
    Yet blithesome as this river
      On which the smiling moonbeams float
      That thus have there for ages smiled,
    And will thus smile for ever.
    And now no more the fresh green-wood,
     The forest's fretted aisles,
    And leafy domes above them bent,
      And solitude
        So eloquent!
    Mocking the varied skill y'-blent
      In Art's most gorgeous piles—
    No more can soothe my soul to sleep
    Than they can awe the sounds that sweep

To hunter's horn and merriment
  Their verdant passes through,
When fresh the dun-deer leaves his scent
  Upon the morning dew.

The game's afoot!—and let the chase
  Lead on, whate'er my destiny—
Though Fate her funeral drum may brace
  Full soon for me!
And wave death's pageant o'er me—
Yet now the new and untried world
Like maiden banner first unfurled,
  Is glancing bright before me!
The quarry soars! and mine is now the sky,
Where, "at what bird I please, my hawk shall fly!"

Yet something whispers through the wood—
  A voice like that perchance
Which taught the hunter of Egeria's grove
To tame the Roman's dominating mood,
  And lower, for awhile, his conquering lance
Before the images of Law and Love—
Some mystic voice that ever since hath dwelt
  Along with Echo in her dim retreat,
A voice whose influence all, at times, have felt
  By wood or glen, or where on silver strand
The clasping waves of Ocean's belt
  Will clashing meet
    Around the land:
It whispers me that soon—too soon
  The pulses which now beat so high,

Impatient with the world to cope,
Will, like the hues of autumn sky,
Be changed and fallen ere life's noon
Should tame its morning hope.

Yet why,
While Hope so jocund singeth
And with her plumes the gray beard's arrow wingeth,
Should I
Think only of the barb it bringeth?
Though every dream deceive
That to my youth is dearest,
Until my heart they leave
Like forest leaf when searest—
Yet still, mid forest leaves
Where now
Its tissue thus my idle fancy weaves,
Still with heart new-blossoming
While leaves, and buds, and wild flowers spring,
At Nature's shrine I'll bow;
Nor seek in vain that truth in her
She keeps for her idolater.

What is Solitude?

NOT in the shadowy wood,
Not in the crag-hung glen,
Not where the echoes brood
In caves untrod by men;

Not by the black seashore,
  Where barren surges break,
Not on the mountain hoar,
  Not by the breezeless lake;
Not on the desert plain
  Where man hath never stood,
Whether on isle or main—
  Not there is solitude.

Birds are in woodland bowers;
  Voices in lonely dells:
Streams to the listening hours
  Talk in earth's secret cells;
Over the gray-ribbed sand
  Breathe Ocean's frothy lips;
Over the still lake's strand
  The wild flower toward it dips;
Pluming the mountain's crest
  Life tosses in its pines,
Coursing the desert's breast
  Life in the steed's mane shines.

Leave—if thou wouldst be lonely—
  Leave Nature for the crowd;
Seek there for one—one only
  With kindred mind endowed!
There—as with Nature erst
  Closely thou wouldst commune—
The deep soul-music nursed
  In either heart, attune!

Heart-wearied thou wilt own,
  Vainly that phantom wooed,
That thou at last hast known
  What is true Solitude!

THE BOB-O-LINKUM.

THOU vocal sprite—thou feather'd troubadour!
  In pilgrim weeds through many a clime a ranger,
Com'st thou to doff thy russet suit once more
  And play in foppish trim the masquing stranger?
Philosophers may teach thy whereabouts and nature;
  But wise, as all of us, perforce, must think 'em,
The school-boy best hath fixed thy nomenclature,
  And poets, too, must call thee Bob-O-Linkum.

Say! art thou, long 'mid forest glooms benighted,
  So glad to skim our laughing meadows over—
With our gay orchards here so much delighted,
  It makes thee musical, thou airy rover?
Or are those buoyant notes the pilfer'd treasure
  Of fairy isles, which thou hast learn'd to ravish
Of all their sweetest minstrelsy at pleasure,
  And, Ariel-like, again on men to lavish?

They tell sad stories of thy mad-cap freaks
  Wherever o'er the land thy pathway ranges;
And even in a brace of wandering weeks,
  They say, alike thy song and plumage changes;

Here both are gay; and when the buds put forth,
  And leafy June is shading rock and river,
Thou art unmatch'd, blithe warbler of the North,
  While through the balmy air thy clear notes quiver

Joyous, yet tender—was that gush of song
  Caught from the brooks, where 'mid its wild
    flowers smiling
The silent prairie listens all day long,
  The only captive to such sweet beguiling;
Or didst thou, flitting through the verdurous halls
  And column'd isles of western groves symphonious,
Learn from the tuneful woods, rare madrigals,
  To make our flowering pastures here harmonious?

Caught'st thou thy carol from Ottawa maid,
  Where, through the liquid fields of wild-rice
    plashing,
Brushing the ears from off the burdened blade,
  Her birch canoe o'er some lone lake is flashing?
Or did the reeds of some savannah south
  Detain thee while thy northern flight pursuing,
To place those melodies in thy sweet mouth,
  The spice-fed winds had taught them in their
    wooing?

Unthrifty prodigal!—is no thought of ill
  Thy ceaseless roundelay disturbing ever?
Or doth each pulse in choiring cadence still
  Throb on in music till at rest for ever?

Yet now in wilder'd maze of concord floating,
'Twould seem that glorious hymning to prolong,
Old Time in hearing thee might fall a-doting,
And pause to listen to thy rapturous song!

PRIMEVAL WOODS.

I.

YES! even here, not less than in the crowd,
Here, where yon vault in formal sweep seems piled
Upon the pines, monotonously proud,
Fit dome for fane, within whose hoary veil
No ribald voice an echo hath defiled—
Where *Silence* seems articulate; up-stealing
Like a low anthem's heavenward wail:—
Oppressive on my bosom weighs the feeling
Of thoughts that language cannot shape aloud;
For song too solemn, and for prayer too wild,—
Thoughts, which beneath no human power could quail,
For lack of utterance, in abasement bow'd—
The cavern'd waves that struggle for revealing,
Upon whose idle foam alone God's light hath smiled.

II.

Ere long thine every stream shall find a tongue,
Land of the Many Waters! But the sound
Of human music, these wild hills among,
Hath no one save the Indian mother flung

Its spell of tenderness? Oh, o'er this ground,
So redolent of *Beauty*, hath there play'd no breath
Of human poesy—none beside the word
Of Love, as, murmur'd these old boughs beneath,
Some fierce and savage suitor it hath bound
To gentle pleadings? Have but these been heard?
No mind, no soul here kindled but my own?
Doth not one hollow trunk about resound
With the faint echoes of a song long flown,
By shadows like itself now haply heard alone?

III.

And Ye, with all this primal growth must go!
And loiterers beneath some lowly spreading shade,
Where pasture-kissing breezes shall, ere then, have
play'd,
A century hence, will doubt that there could grow
From that meek land such Titans of the glade!
Yet wherefore *primal?* when beneath my tread
Are roots whose thrifty growth, perchance, hath
arm'd
The Anak spearman when his trump alarm'd;
Roots that the Deluge wave hath plunged below;
Seeds that the Deluge wind hath scattered;
Berries that Eden's warblers may have fed;
In slime of earlier worlds preserved unharmed,
Again to quicken, germinate, and blow,
Again to charm the land as erst the land they
charm'd.

THE STREAMLET.

HOW silently yon streamlet slides
   From out the twilight-shaded bowers!
How, soft as sleep, it onward glides
   In sunshine through its dreaming flowers.

That tranquil wave, now turn'd to gold
   Beneath the slowly westering sun,
It is the same, far on the wold,
   Whose foam this morn we gazed upon.

The leaden sky, the barren waste,
   The torrent we this morning knew,
How changed are all! as now we haste
   To bid them, with the day, adieu!

Ah! thus should life and love at last
   Grow bright and sweet when death is near:
May we, our course of trial pass'd,
   Thus bathed in beauty glide from here!

A HUNTER'S MATIN.

UP, comrades, up, the morn's awake
   Upon the mountain side,
The curlew's wing hath swept the lake,
And the deer has left the tangled brake,
   To drink from the limpid tide.
Up, comrades, up! the mead-lark's note
And the plover's cry o'er the prairie float,

The squirrel he springs from his covert now
To prank it away on the chestnut bough,
Where the oriole's pendent nest high up,
Is rock'd on the swaying trees,
While the humbird sips from the harebell's cup,
As it bends to the morning breeze.
Up, comrades, up! our shallops grate
Upon the pebbly strand,
And our stalwart hounds impatient wait
To spring from the huntsman's hand.

My Birchen Bark.

MY birchen bark, my birchen bark!
When Fortune first made Love a rover,
He shaped it for his own trim ark
To float Care's deluge gayly over.
Then leave the boasting pioneer
To hew his skiff from yonder pine,
And, dearest, with young Love to steer,
Become a passenger in mine:
In swan-like grace thy form resembling—
With joy beneath thy sweet limbs trembling—
For lightsome heart, oh, such a boat
On summer wave did never float!

Think'st thou, my love, that painted barge,
With gaudy pennant flaunting o'er her,
Could kiss, like her, the flowery marge,
Nor break the foam-bells formed before her?

Look, sweet, the very lotus-cup,
  Trembling as if with bliss o'erbrimm'd,
Seemed now almost to buoy her up
  As o'er the heart-shaped leaves we skimm'd—
Those floating hearts, beside their flowers,
Half bear the boat and both of ours !
For lightsome heart, oh, such a boat
On summer wave did never float !

The Brook and the Pine.

TELL me, fair Brook, that long hast sung,
  To yonder Pine hast sung so sweetly—
Are its wild arms more near thee flung,
  When night their motion veils completely?
Or, for the morn's caressing rays
  Still eager, will it toss its boughs,—
Like hearts that only beat for praise,
  All heedless of affection's vows?

I never pause—the Brook replied—
  To know how near it bends above me,
I cannot help, whate'er betide,
  To sing for one I fain would love me;
My song flows on, and still must flow,
  My chosen Pine with truth to bless,
Though rippling pebbles sometimes show
  The brook athirst with tenderness:

Nay more—when thus, while troublous, oft
  My wavelets flash some ray redeeming,

I think but of the Pine aloft,
Which first will proudly hail its beaming!
And, wasted thus, a joy it is
To know my Pine,—refresh'd and bright,
While I distill'd each dewy kiss—
Is worthy of all glorious light!

The Western Hunter to his Mistress.

WEND, love, with me, to the deep woods wend,
Where far in the forest the wild flowers keep,
Where no watching eye shall over us bend,
Save the blossoms that into thy bower may peep.
Thou shalt gather from buds of the oriole's hue,
Whose flaming wings round our pathway flit,
From the saffron orchis and lupin blue,
And those like the foam on my courser's bit.

One steed and one saddle us both shall bear,
One hand of each on the bridle meet;
And beneath the wrist that entwines me there,
An answering pulse from my heart shall beat.
I will sing thee many a joyous lay,
As we chase the deer by the blue lake-side,
While the winds that over the prairie play
Shall fan the cheek of my woodland bride.

Our home shall be by the cool, bright streams,
Where the beaver chooses her safe retreat,
And our hearth shall smile like the sun's warm gleams
Through the branches around our lodge that meet.

Then wend with me, to the deep woods wend,
  Where far in the forest the wild flowers keep,
Where no watching eye shall over us bend,
  Save the blossoms that into thy bower may peep.

A Frontier Incident.

THE Indian whoop is heard without,
  Within the Indian arrow lies;
There's horror in that fiendish shout,
  There's death where'er that arrow flies.

Two trembling women there alone,
  Alone to guard a feeble child;
What shield, O God! is round them thrown
  Amid that scene of peril wild?

Thy Book upon the table there
  Reveals at once from whence could flow
The strength to dash aside despair,
  The meekness to abide the blow.

Already, half resign'd, she kneels,
  And half imploring, kneels the mother,
Awhile angelic courage steels
  The gentle nature of the other.

They thunder on the oaken door,
  They pierce the air with furious yell,
And soon that plume upon the floor
  May grace some painted warrior well.

Oh, why cannot one stalwart arm
  But wield the brand that hangeth by?
And snatch the noble girl from harm,
  Who heedeth not the hellish cry?

A shot! the savage leader falls—
  The maiden's eye which aim'd the gun—
That eye, whose deadly aim appals,
  Is tearful when its task is done.

He falls—and straight with baffled cries,
  His tribesmen fly in wild dismay;
And now, beneath the evening skies,
  That Household may in safety pray.

The Laurel.

BELIEVE him not, that rhyming, rakish Roman,
  Who swore so roundly that a lover's quarrel
Between one Phœbus and some thick-shod woman,
  First caused to sprout the leaflets of the laurel!

Why, long ago,—ere his Deucalion floated
  Upon that freshet, which was so surprising
In that small world where every rill is noted,
  As if it were a Mississippi rising:

Yes, long ere then, on ALLEGHAN's bright mountains,
  Na-nabozho had seen the laurel growing,
With berries glassed in Adirondach fountains,
  Or cup mist-filled near Niagara's flowing:

A crimped and dainty cup, whose timid flushing
  Tinted the creamy hue of lips so shrinking,
He thought at first some sentient thing was blushing,
  To be thus caught from such a caldron thinking.

Plants then had tongues,—if we believe old story,
  As told by red men under forest branches,—
(Who still insist they hear that language hoary,
  Ere mountain-woods descend in avalanches.*)

Plants then had tongues, and in their careless tattle,
  Each painted creature on its footstalk swaying,
Beguiled the loitering hunter, with their prattle,
  Secrets of Nature and old Earth betraying.

And once, they said, when Earth seemed fully freighted
  With pearly cup, and star, and tufted blossom,
A Mohawk youth, with spirit all unmated,
  On old Ta-ha-was† flung his weary bosom.

He knew not, could not, comprehend the feeling
  That kept him mute oppressed with thought unuttered,
That wild, wild sense of loveliness o'erstealing
  Which urged his pent soul forth on wing unfettered.

* Forest Avalanches, or "Mountain Slides," are said to be preceded by a strange groaning of the trees. It is probably, however, only the *grinding* of the loosened ground beneath them.

† The high peak of the Adirondachs, in whose side is the fountain-head of the Hudson.

Despairing and bewildered in his sorrow,
  He pressed with quivering lip the hollow mountain,
As he its giant hardihood would borrow,
  Its free-voiced rushing wind and chainless fountain.

This for a savage to be sure was tender,—
  Whose hottest passion chiefly for the chase is:
And when his native soil refused to render
  Aught of response to her wild son's embraces,—

He breathed into the ground vague thoughts of power,
  The yearnings of a soul in silence hidden;
Beneath the midnight sky in that lone hour,
  Thought found a language by itself unbidden!

Then, with no human eye its birth beholding,
  No fostering plaudit human hands bestowing,
First to the dew its glossy leaves unfolding,
  Sprouted the Laurel, from its own heart growing.

And still that type of native genius telleth,
  On barren rock, or lonely woodland bower,
Not in *approval*, but in *Utterance* dwelleth
  The Poet's craving, and the Poet's power.

THE AMBUSCADE.

A TRADITION OF LAKE IROQUOIS, OR CHAMPLAIN.

THE mountain-tops are bright above,
The lake is bright beneath—
And the mist is seen, the rocks between,
In a silver shroud to wreathe.
Merrily on the maple spray
The redbreast trills his roundelay,
And the oriole blithely flits among
The boughs where her pendent nest is hung:
The squirrel his morning revel keeps
In the chestnut's leafy screen,
And the fawn from the thicket gayly leaps
To gambol upon the green.
Now on the broad lake's waters blue
Dances many a light canoe;
And banded there, in wampum sheen,
Many a crested chief is seen;
Now as the foamy fringe they break,
Which the waves, where they kiss the margin, make,
The shallops shoot on the snowy strand,
And the plumed warriors leap to land.

They bear their pirogues of birchen bark
Far in the shadowy forest glade,
And plunge them deep in covert dark
Of the closely-woven hazel shade;
Then stealthily tread in each other's track,
And with wary step come gliding back.

And when the water again is won,
Unlace the beaded moccason,
And covering first with careful hand
The footmarks dash'd in the yielding sand,
Round jutting point and dented bay
Through the wave they take their winding way.

Awhile their painted forms are seen
Gleaming along the margin green,
And then the sunny lake is left—
Where issuing from a mountain cleft—
Above whose bold impending height
The dusky larch excludes the light,
The current of a rivulet
Conceals their wary footsteps yet.

Scaling the rocks, where strong and deep
Abrupt the waters foaming leap,
Along the stream they bending creep,
Where the hanging birch's tassels sweep,
Thrid the witch-hazel and alder-maze,
Where in broken rills the streamlet strays,
And reach the spot where its oozy tide
Steals from the mountain's shaggy side.

Now where wild vines their tendrils fling,
From crag to crag their forms they swing,
Some boldly find a footing where
The mountain cat would hardly dare;
Others as lightly onward bound
As the frolic chipmonk skips the ground,

Till all the midway mountain gain
  And there once more collected meet,
Where on the eagle's wild domain
  The morning sunbeams fiercely beat.

There's a glen upon that mountain-side,
A sunny dell expanding wide,
Where the eye that looks through the green arcade
Of cliffs in vines and shrubs array'd,
Sees many a silver stream and lake
Upon its raptured vision break ;
That sunny dell has its opening bright
Almost within an arrow's flight
Of a fearful gorge whose upper side
Rank weeds and furze as closely hide,
As if Pau-puck-wis there had plied
  His skill in weaving osiers green,
And thus in thievish freak had tried
  Its gloomy mouth to screen.

'Tis a chasm beneath the wooded steep,
Where the brain will swim and the blood will creep
  When its dizzy edge is seen,
And the Fiend will prompt the heart to leap
When the eye would measure the yawning deep
  Of that hideous ravine !
Far down the gulf in distance dim
The bat will oft at noontide skim,
The rattlesnake like a shadow glides
Through poisonous weeds in its shelvy sides,

While swarming lizards loathsome crawl
Where the green-damp stands on the slimy wall,
And the venomous copper-snake's heard to hiss
On the frightful edge of that black abyss.

Here, in the feathery fern—between
The tangled thicket's matted screen,
Their weapons hid, save where a blade
From straggling ray reflection made,
  The Adirondach warriors lay.
The morning sees them gather there
And crouch within their leafy lair—
  The scorching beams of noontide hour,
If boughs should lift, would only play
On bronzed and motionless array
  Within that silent bower:
Still silent when the mantle gray
  Of sombre twilight slowly fell
  O'er rocky height and wooded dell,
Those men of bronze all silent they
Still waited for their prey!

How slow the languid moments move,
  How long to him their lapse appears
In whom remorse, or fear, or love,
  Concentres griefs untold by tears,
  The gather'd agony of years!
But o'er the Indian warrior's soul
Uncounted and unheeded roll
  Long hours, like these in watching spent,

The moments that he knows within,
  When on the glorious War-Path sent,
Are calm as those which usher in
The thunders of the firmament!

The moose hath left the rushy brink
Where he stole to the lake at eve to drink,
And sought his lair in thicket dark,
Lit only by the fire-fly's spark.
Now myriad stars are twinkling through
The vaulted heaven's veil of blue,
And seen reflected in the wave
With golden studs its bed to pave.
Now as upon the western hills
The moon her mystic circle fills,
Against the sky each cliff is flung,
As if at magic touch it sprung;
And as the wood her beam receives,
  The dewdrop in that virgin light
Pendent from the quivering leaves,
  Sparkles upon the pall of night.

Deep in the linden's foliage hid,
Complains the peevish katydid,
And the shrill screech-owl answers back
From tulip tree and tamarack.
At times along the placid lake
A solitary trout will break,
And rippling eddies on the stream
In trembling circles faintly gleam;
While near the sedgy shore is heard
The plash of that ill-omen'd bird,

Whose dismal note and boding cry
  Will oft the startled ear assail,
When lowering clouds obscure the sky,
And when the tempest gathers nigh
  Come quivering in the rising gale.

Oh, why cannot that loon's wild shriek
To them a feeble warning speak,
Whose proudly waving banner now
Comes floating round the mountain brow,
Whose gallant ranks in close array
Now gleam along the moonlit way;
And now with many a break between,
Are winding through the long ravine?

Oh, why cannot that loon's wild shriek
To them a feeble warning speak,
Who careless press a foeman's sod
As if in banquet-hall they trod;
Who rashly thus undaunted dare
  To chase in woods the forest child,
To hunt the panther to his lair,
  The Indian in his native wild?

Unapprehensive thus, at night
  The wild doe looking from the brake,
To where there gleams a fitful light
  Dotted upon the rippling lake,
Sees not the silver spray-drop dripping
From the lithe oar which, softly dipping,

Impels the wily hunter's boat;
But on his ruddy torch's rays,
As nearer, clearer now they float,
The fated quarry stands to gaze,
And dreaming not of cruel sport,
Withdraws not thence her gentle eyes
Until the rifle's sharp report
The simple creature hears and dies.

Buoyant with youth, as heedless they
Pursue the death-besetted way,
As cautionless each one proceeds,
Where his doom'd steps the pathway leads,
As if the peril of that hour
But led those steps to beauty's bower.
They come with stirring fife and drum,
With flaunting plume and pennon come,
To solitudes where never yet
Hath gleamed the glistening bayonet—
Banner upon the breeze hath flown,
Or bugle note before been blown.
The cautious beaver starts with fear,
That strange unwonted sound to hear;
But still her grave demeanor keeps,
As from her hovel-door she peeps—
Observing thence with curious eye
The pageant as it passes by;
Pauses the wailing whipporwill
One moment, in her plaintive trill,
As echoing on the mountain-side
Their martial music wanders wide;

Then, as the last note dies away,
Pursues once more her broken lay.

At length they reach that fatal steep,
Which, hanging o'er the chasm deep,
With stunted copse and tangled heath,
Conceals the gulf that yawns beneath.
The watchful Indian, from his lair,
One moment sees them falter there—
One moment looks, with eagle eye,
To mark their forms against the sky;
Then through the night air, wild and high,
Peals the red warrior's battle cry.

From sassafras and sumac green,
From shatter'd stump, and riven rock—
From the dark hemlock boughs between
Is launch'd the gleaming tomahawk.
And savage eyes glare fiercely out
From every bush and vine about;
And savage forms the branches throw
In dusky masses on the foe.

In vain their leaders strive to form
Their ranks beneath that living storm!
As whoop on whoop discordant fell
Loudly on their astounded ears,
As if at once each fiendish yell
Awoke, within that narrow dell,
The echoes of a thousand years!
No rallying cry, no hoarse command
Can marshal that bewilder'd band;

Nor clarion-call to standard, more
Those panic-stricken ranks restore ;
Now strown like pines upon the path
Where bursts the fierce tornado's wrath.

Yet some there are who undismay'd
Seek sternly, back to back array'd,
With eye and blade alert, in vain
A moment's footing to maintain.
Though gallant hearts direct the steel,
And stalwart arms the buffets deal,
What can a score of brands avail
When each as many foes assail !
Like scud before the wintry blast,
That through the sky comes sweeping fast,
Like leaves upon the tempest whirl'd
They toward the steep are struggling hurl'd.

Valor in vain, in vain despair
Nerves many a frantic bosom there,
Furious with the unequal strife,
To cling with desperate force to life.
There, fighting still, with mad endeavor,
As on the dizzy edge they hover,
Their bugle breathes one rallying note,
Pennon and plume one moment float ;
Then, swept beyond the frightful brink
Like mist, into the chasm sink ;
Within whose bosom as they fell,
Arose as hideous, wild a yell
As if the very earth were riven,
And shrieks from hell were upward driven.

Away to the Forest.

AWAY to the forest, away, love, away!
My foam-champing courser reproves thy delay,
And the brooks are all calling, Away, love, away!
Away to the forest, my own love, with me!
Away where thro' checker'd glade sports the wind free,
Where in the bosky dell
Watching young leaflets swell,
Spring on each floral bell
Counteth for thee
Away to the forest, away!

Away to the forest, away, love, away!
Each breath of the morning reproves thy delay;
Each shadow retiring beckons away!
Hark! how the blue-bird's throat carolling o'er us
Chimes with the thrush's note floating before us!
Away then, my gentle one,
Thy voice is miss'd alone.
Away—let love's whisper'd tone
Swell the bright chorus,
Away to the forest, away!

INDIAN SUMMER, 1828.

LIGHT as love's smile the silvery mist at morn
  Floats in loose flakes along the limpid river;
The blue-bird's notes upon the soft breeze borne,
  As high in air he carols, faintly quiver;
The weeping birch, like banners idly waving,
Bends to the stream, its spicy branches laving,
  Beaded with dew the witch-elm's tassels shiver;
The timid rabbit from the furze is peeping,
And from the springy spray the squirrel gayly leaping.

I love thee, Autumn, for thy scenery, ere
  The blasts of winter chase the varied dyes
That richly deck the slow declining year;
  I love the splendor of thy sunset skies,
The gorgeous hues that tint each failing leaf
Lovely as beauty's cheek, as woman's love too, brief;
  I love the note of each wild bird that flies,
As on the wind he pours his parting lay,
And wings his loitering flight to summer climes away.

O Nature! fondly I still turn to thee
  With feelings fresh as e'er my chilhood's were;
Though wild and passion-tost my youth may be,
  Toward thee I still the same devotion bear;
To thee—to thee—though health and hope no more
Life's wasted verdure may to me restore—
  Still—still, childlike I come, as when in prayer

I bowed my head upon a mother's knee,
And deem'd the world, like her, all truth and purity.

The Language of Flowers.

TEACH thee their language! sweet, I know no tongue,
No mystic art those gentle things declare,
I ne'er could trace the schoolman's trick among
Created things, so delicate and rare:
Their language? Prythee! why they are themselves
But bright thoughts syllabled to shape and hue,
The tongue that erst was spoken by the elves,
When tenderness as yet within the world was new.

And oh, do not their soft and starry eyes—
Now bent to earth, to heaven now meekly pleading—
Their incense fainting as it seeks the skies,
Yet still from earth with freshening hope receding—
Say, do not these to every heart declare,
With all the silent eloquence of truth,
The language that they speak is Nature's prayer,
To give her back those spotless days of youth?

"*Where would I Rest?*"

UNDER old boughs, where moist the livelong summer
The moss is green, and springy to your tread,
When you, my friend, shall be an often comer
To pierce the thicket, seeking for my bed:

For thickets heavy all around should screen it
From careless gazer that might wander near,
Nor even to him who by some chance had seen it,
Would I have aught to catch his eye, appear:

One lonely stem—a trunk those old boughs lifting,
Should mark the spot; and, haply, new thrift owe
To that which upward through its sap was drifting
From what lay mouldering round its roots below.

There my freed spirit with the dawn's first gleaming
Would come to revel round the dancing spray:
There would it linger with the day's last beaming,
To watch thy footsteps thither track their way.

The quivering leaf should whisper in that hour
Things that for thee alone would have a sound,
And parting boughs my spirit-glances shower
In gleams of light upon the mossy ground.

There, when long years and all thy journeyings over—
Loosed from this world thyself to join the free,

Thou too wouldst come to rest beside thy lover
In that sweet cell beneath our Trysting-Tree.

Morning Hymn.

"LET there be light!" The Eternal spoke,
And from the abyss where darkness rode
The earliest dawn of nature broke,
And light around creation flow'd.
The glad earth smiled to see the day,
The first-born day, come blushing in;
The young day smiled to shed its ray
Upon a world untouch'd by sin.

"Let there be light!" O'er heaven and earth,
The God who first the day-beam pour'd,
Utter'd again his fiat forth,
And shed the Gospel's light abroad.
And, like the dawn, its cheering rays
On rich and poor were meant to fall,
Inspiring their Redeemer's praise
In lowly cot and lordly hall.

Then come, when in the Orient first
Flushes the signal light for prayer;
Come with the earliest beams that burst
From God's bright throne of glory there.
Come kneel to Him who through the night
Hath watch'd above thy sleeping soul,
To Him, whose mercies, like his light,
Are shed abroad from pole to pole.

Room, Boys, Room.

THERE was an old hunter camp'd down by the rill,
Who fish'd in this water, and shot on that hill.
The forest for him had no danger, nor gloom,
For all that he wanted was plenty of room!
Says he, "The world's wide, there is room for us all;
Room enough in the green-wood, if not in the hall.
Room, boys, room, by the light of the moon,
For why shouldn't every man enjoy his own room?"

He wove his own nets, and his shanty was spread
With the skins he had dress'd and stretch'd out overhead;
Fresh branches of hemlock made fragrant the floor,
For his bed, as he sung when the daylight was o'er,
"The world's wide enough, there is room for us all;
Room enough in the green-wood, if not in the hall.
Room, boys, room, by the light of the moon,
For why shouldn't every man enjoy his own room?"

That spring now half choked by the dust of the road,
Under boughs of old maples once limpidly flow'd;
By the rock whence it bubbles his kettle was hung,
Which their sap often fill'd, while the hunter he sung,
"The world's wide enough, there is room for us all;
Room enough in the green-wood, if not in the hall.
Room, boys, room, by the light of the moon,
For why shouldn't every man enjoy his own room?"

And still sung the hunter—when one gloomy day,
He saw in the forest what sadden'd his lay,—
A heavy-wheel'd wagon its black rut had made,
Where fair grew the greensward in broad forest
glade—
"The world's wide enough, there is room for us all;
Room enough in the green-wood, if not in the hall.
Room, boys, room, by the light of the moon,
For why shouldn't every man enjoy his own room?"

He whistled his dog, and says he, "We can't stay;
I must shoulder my rifle, up traps, and away."
Next day, through those maples the settler's axe rung,
While slowly the hunter trudged off as he sung,
"The world's wide enough, there is room for us all;
Room enough in the green-wood, if not in the hall.
Room, boys, room, by the light of the moon,
For why shouldn't every man enjoy his own room?"

LAYS OF THE HUDSON.

"—Thou didst hear the far off Ocean sound,
Inviting thee from hill and vale away,
To mingle thy deep waters with its own;
And at that voice thy steps did onward glide,
Onward from echoing hill and valley lone—
Like thine oh be my course! nor turned aside
While listing to the soundings of a land
That, like the ocean-call, invites me to its strand."

Mrs. Oakes Smith's *Sonnet to the Hudson.*

Lays of the Hudson.

To the Hudson River.

RIVER, O river, thou rovest free
From the mountain height to the fresh blue sea,
Free thyself, while in silver chain
Linking each charm of land and main.
Calling at first thy banded waves
From hill-side thickets and fern-hid caves,
From the splinter'd crag thou leap'st below,
Through leafy glades at will to flow—
Idling now 'mid the dallying sedge,
Slumbering now by the steep's moss'd edge,
With statelier march once more to break
From wooded valley to breezy lake;
Yet all of these scenes, though fair they be,
River, O river, are bann'd to me!

River, O river! upon thy tide
Gayly the freighted vessels glide;
Would that thou thus couldst bear away
The thoughts that burthen my weary day,
Or that I, from all, save them, set free,
Though laden still, might rove with thee.

True that thy waves brief lifetime find,
And live at the will of the wanton wind—
True that thou seekest the ocean's flow
To be lost therein for evermoe!
Yet the slave who worships at Glory's shrine,
But toils for a bubble as frail as thine,
But loses his freedom here, to be
Forgotten as soon as in death set free.

---

*MOONLIGHT UPON THE HUDSON.**

WRITTEN AT WEST POINT.

I'M not romantic, but, upon my word,
  There are some moments when one can't help feeling
As if his heart's chords were so strongly stirr'd
  By things around him, that 'tis vain concealing;
A little music in his soul still lingers,
Whene'er its keys are touch'd by Nature's fingers.

And even here upon this settee lying
  With many a sleepy traveller near me snoozing,
Thoughts warm and wild are through my bosom flying,
  Like founts when first into the sunshine oozing:
For who can look on mountain, sky and river,
Like these, and then be calm and cold as ever!

* Written in the baggage-room while waiting for the steamboat.

Bright DIAN, who, Camilla-like, dost skim yon
Azure fields—Thou who, once earthward bending,
Didst loose thy virgin zone to young Endymion,
On dewy Latmos to his arms descending—
Thou whom the world of old on every shore,
Type of thy sex, *Triformis*, did adore:

Tell me—where'er thy silver bark be steering,
By bright Italian or soft Persian lands,
Or o'er those island-studded seas careering,
Whose pearl-charged waves dissolve on coral strands;
Tell if thou visitest, thou heavenly rover,
A lovelier stream than this the wide world over?

Doth Achelous or Araxes flowing
Twin-born from Pindus, but ne'er meeting brothers—
Doth Tagus o'er his golden pavement glowing,
Or cradle-freighted Ganges, the reproach of mothers,
The storied Rhine, or far-famed Guadalquivir—
Match they in beauty my own glorious river?

What though no cloister gray nor ivied column
Along these cliffs their sombre ruins rear!
What though no frowning tower nor temple solemn
Of tyrants tell and superstition here—
What though that mouldering fort's fast crumbling walls
Did ne'er enclose a baron's banner'd halls—

Its sinking arches once gave back as proud
  An echo to the war-blown clarion's peal,
As gallant hearts its battlements did crowd
  As ever beat beneath a vest of steel,
When herald's trump or knighthood's haughtiest day
Call'd forth chivalric host to battle fray:

For here amid these woods he once kept court
  Before whose mighty soul the common crowd
Of heroes, who alone for fame have fought,
  Are like the patriarch's sheaves to heaven's chosen
      bow'd—
HE who his country's eagle taught to soar,
And fired those stars which shine o'er every shore.

And sights and sounds at which the world have
      wonder'd
  Within these wild ravines have had their birth;
Young FREEDOM'S cannon from these glens have
      thunder'd,
  And sent their startling voices o'er the earth;
And not a verdant glade nor mountain hoary
But treasures up within the glorious story.

And yet not rich in high-soul'd memories only
  Is every moon-kiss'd headland round me gleaming,
Each cavern'd glen and leafy valley lonely,
  And silver torrent o'er the bald rock streaming;
But such soft fancies here may breathe around,
As make Vaucluse and Clarens hallow'd ground.

Where, tell me where, pale watcher of the night—
Thou that to love so oft has lent its soul,
Since the lorn Lesbian languish'd 'neath thy light,
  Or fated Romeo to his Juliet stole—
Where dost thou find a fitter place on earth
To nurse young love in hearts like theirs to birth?

Oh, loiter not upon that fairy shore
  To watch the lazy barks in distance glide,
When sunset brightens on their sails no more,
  And stern-lights twinkle in the dusky tide;
Loiter not there, young heart, at that soft hour,
What time the Queen of Night proclaims love's power.

Even as I gaze, upon my memory's track
  Bright as yon coil of light along the deep,
A scene of early youth comes dream-like back,
  Where two stand gazing from the tide-wash'd steep,
A sanguine stripling, just toward manhood flushing,
A girl, scarce yet in ripen'd beauty blushing.

The hour is his! and while his hopes are soaring
  Doubts he that maiden will become his bride?
Can she resist that gush of wild adoring
  Fresh from a heart full-volumed as the tide?
Tremulous, but radiant, is that peerless daughter
Of loveliness, as is the star-strown water!

The moist leaves glimmer as they glimmer'd then,
  Alas! how oft have they been since renew'd,
How oft the whippoorwill, from yonder glen,
  Each year has whistled to her callow brood,

How oft have lovers by yon star's same gleam,
Dream'd here of bliss—and waken'd from their dream!

But now, bright Peri of the skies, descending
 Thy pearly car hangs o'er yon mountain crest,
And night, more nearly now each step attending,
 As if to hide thy envied place of rest,
Closes at last thy very couch beside,
A matron curtaining a virgin bride.

Farewell! Though tears on every leaf are starting,
 While through the shadowy boughs thy glances quiver,
As of the good, when heavenward hence departing,
 Shines thy last smile upon the placid river,
So—could I fling o'er glory's tide one ray—
Would I too steal from this dark world away.

KACHESCO.

A LEGEND OF THE SOURCES OF THE HUDSON.

He held him with his glittering eye.—COLERIDGE.

L'ENVOY.

THE fragile bark whereon the Indian traces
 Rude tokens of his path for other eyes,
Sometimes outlasts the tree on which he places
Anew the birchen scroll he thence had peeled,
And while he wanders forth to other skies,
Some curious Settler, ere his axe he wield,

The frail memorial careful bears away :—
So I have freely traced a woodland lay,
In lines as quaint as chart of forest child,
Content, like him, if, passing on my way,
I cheer some friendly heart in life's dull wild,
A birchen scroll from birchen tree y'cleft,
A trail of moccasin in wildering forest left.

PART I.—"CAMPING OUT."

I.

'Twas in the mellow autumn time,
That revel of our masquing clime,
When, as the Indian crone believes,
The rainbow tints of Nature's prime
She in her forest banner weaves ;
To show, in that bright blazonry,
How the young earth did first supply
Each gorgeous hue that paints the sky,
Or in the sunset billow heaves.

II.

'Twas in the mellow autumn time,
When, from the spongy, swollen swamp,
The lake a darker tide receives ;
When nights are growing long and damp ;
And at the dawn a glistering rime
Is silver'd o'er the gaudy leaves ;
When hunters leave their hill-side camp,
With fleet hound some, the dun-deer rousing,
In "still-hunt" some, to shoot him browsing ;

And close at night their forest tramp,
    Where the fat yearling scents their fire,
And, new unto their murderous ways,
    Affrighted, feels his life expire
As stupidly he stands at gaze,
    Where that wild crew sit late carousing.

III.

'Twas in the mellow autumn time,
    When I, an idler from the town,
With gun and rod was lured to climb
  Those peaks where fresh the HUDSON takes
  His tribute from an hundred lakes;
    Lakes which the sun, though pouring down
His mid-day splendors round each isle,
  At eventide so soon forsakes
That you may watch his fading smile
    For hours around those summits glow
    When all is gray and chill below;
While, in that brief autumnal day
Still, varying all in future, they
    Will yet some wilding beauty show,
As through their watery maze you stray.

IV.

  For he beholds, whose footfalls press
  The mosses of that wilderness,
Each charm the glorious HUDSON boasts
    Through his far-reaching strand—
When, sweeping from these leafy coasts,

His mighty march he seaward takes—
First pictured in those mountain lakes,
All fresh from Nature's hand!
Lakes broadly flashing to the sun,
Like warrior's shield when first display'd,
Lakes, dark, as when, the battle done,
That shield oft blackens in the glade.
Round one that on the eye will ope
With many a winding sunny reach,
The rising hills all gently slope
From turfy bank and pebbled beach.
With rocks and ragged forests bound,
Deep set in fir-clad mountain shade,
You trace another, where resound
The echoes of the hoarse cascade.

V.

Aweary with a day of toil,
And all uncheer'd with hunter spoil,
Guiding a wet and sodden boat,
With thing, half paddle, half an oar,
I chanced, one murky eve, to float
Along the grim and ghastly shore
Of such wild water;
Past trees, some shooting from the bank,
With dead boughs dipping in the wave,
And some with trunks moss-grown and dank,
On which the savage, that here drank
A thousand years ago, might grave
His tale of slaughter.

VI.

Peering amid these mouldering stems,
Through thickets from their ruins starting,
To spy a deer-track if I could,
I saw the boughs before me parting,
Revealing what seemed two bright gems
Gleaming from out the dusky wood;
And in that moment on the shore,
Just where I brush'd it with my oar,
An aged INDIAN stood!

VII.

Nay! shrink not, lady, from my tale,
Because, erst moved by border story,
Thy thoughtful cheek grew still more pale
At images so dire and gory;
Nor yet—grown colder since that day—
Cry—half disdainful of my lay,
"An INDIAN!—why, in theme so stale,
There can be no new interest! *can* there?—
'Twas but some border vagrant gazing
From thicket that your boat was grazing,
And you—you took him for a panther!"

VIII.

It was just so, and nothing more;
The deer-stand that I sought was here,
Here too Kachesco came for deer;
A civil Indian, seldom drunk,
Who dragg'd my leaky skiff ashore,
And pointed out a fallen trunk,

Where sitting I could spy the brink,
Beneath the gently tilting branches,
And shoot the buck that came to drink
Or wash the black-flies from his haunches.
With this he plunged into the wood,
Saying he on the "run-way" knew
Another stand, and quite as good
If but the night breeze fairly blew.

IX.

So there, like mummied sagamore,
I crouch with senses fairly aching,
To catch each sound by wood or shore
Upon the twilight stillness breaking.
I start! that crash of leaves below
A light hoof surely rattles?—No!
From overhead a dry branch parted.
A plash! 'Tis but the wavelet tapping
Yon floating log. The partridge drums;
With thrilling ears again I've started;
The booming sound at distance hums
Like rushing herds. I start as though
A gang of moose had caught me napping.
And now my straining sight grows dim
While nearer yet the night-hawks skim;
Well, "let the hart ungalled play,"
I'll think of sweet looks far away—
But no! I list and gaze about,
My rifle to my shoulder clapping
At leap of every rascal trout,
Or lotus leaf the water flapping.

X.

An hour went thus, without a sign
Of buck or doe in range appearing;
The wind began to crisp the lake,
The wolf to howl from out the brake,
And I to think that boat of mine
Had better soon be campward steering;
When near me, through the deepening night,
Again I saw those eyes so bright,
And as my swarthy friend drew nigher,
I heard these words pronounced in tone,
Lady, as silken as thine own,
"White man, we'd better make a fire."

XI.

Our kindling-stuff lay near at hand—
Peelings of bark, some half uncoil'd
In flakes, from boughs by age despoil'd,
And some in shreds by rude winds torn;
Dead vines that round the dead trees clung;
Long moss that from their old arms swung,
Tatter'd and stain'd—all weather-worn,
Like funeral weeds hung out to dry,
Or banners drooping mournfully:—
These quickly caught the spark we fann'd.
Branches, that once waved overhead,
Now crisply crackling to our tread,
Fed next the greedy flame's demand.
Lastly a fallen trunk or two—
Which from its weedy lair we drew,
And o'er the blazing brushwood threw—
For savory broil supplied the brand.

XII.

Of hemlock fir we made our couch,
A bed for cramps and colds consoling;
I had some biscuit in my pouch,
A salmon-trout I'd kill'd in trolling;
My comrade had some venison dried,
And corn in bear's lard lately fried;
And on my word, I will avouch
That when we would our stock divide
In equal portions, save the last,
Apicius could not deride
The relish of that night's repast.

XIII.

We talk'd that night—I love to talk
With these grown children of the wild,
When in their native forest walk,
Confiding, simple as a child,
They lose at times that sullen mood
Which marks the wanderer of the wood,
And in that pliant hour will show
As prodigal and fresh of thought
As genius when its feelings flow
In words by feeling only taught.

XIV.

And much he told of *Metai** lore;
Of WABENOS we call enchanters;

* Wizard.—See Notes on Indian Mythology at the end of the volume.

Of water sprites called Nebanai—
In floating logs oft packed away,
As much at home on every shore
As other "spirits" in decanters.
From him I learned of NABOZHOO,*
The Harlequin of Indian story
(A kind of half Deucalion, too,
Who beats the Greek one in his glory);
And of the pigmy WEENG, whose tap
Upon the forehead, near one's peepers,
Will make the liveliest hunter nap
As soundly as The Seven Sleepers;
And of the huge WEENDIGO race
(The Cyclopes of Red-skin fable),
Whose housewives for their breakfast place
A whole cooked Indian on the table.

XV.

Much of PA-PUCK-WIS too he said,
The urchin god of fun and trickery,
And other godlings by him led,
And demons dancing on the head,
As supple as a sapling hickory.
And looking toward The Milky Way,
Which he The Path of Spirits named,
He told how half the soul would stay
Around its early haunts to play,
When God the other half had claimed;
And how all living Red men stand
With half their shade in shadow land;

*For explanation of Indian names see notes on Kachesco.

And how *all Life* to Red men known
Once walked in shapes just like our own;
And though doomed now as brutes to walk,
How Spirits still to brutes will talk,
And whisper blessed words of cheer
From bush or tree they're browsing near,
Saying that *none* at last shall go
Down to the Fiend MACHINETO.

XVI.

We talk'd—'twas next of fish and game,
Of hunter arts to strike the quarry,
Of portages and lakes whose name,
As utter'd in his native speech,
If memory could have hoarded each,
A portage-labor 'twere to carry.
Yet one whose length—it is a score
Of miles perhaps in length, or more—
'Tis glorious to troll,
I can recall the name and feature
From dull oblivion's scathe,
Partly because in trim canoe
I since have track'd it through and through,
Partly that from this simple creature
I heard that night a tale of faith
Which moved my very soul.

XVII.

Yes, INCA-PAH-CO! though thy name
Has never flow'd in poet's numbers,

And all unknown, thy virgin claim
To wild and matchless beauty, slumbers;
Yet memory's pictures all must fade
Ere I forget that sunset view
When, issuing first from darksome glade
A day of storms had darker made,
Thy floating isles and mountains blue,
Thy waters sparkling far away
Round craggy point and verdant bay—
The point with dusky cedars crown'd,
The bay with beach of silver bound—
Upon my raptured vision grew.
Grew every moment, brighter, fairer,
As I, at close of that wild day,
Emerging from the forest nearer,
Saw the red sun his glorious path
Cleave through the storm-cloud's dying wrath,
And with one broad triumphant ray
Upon thy crimson'd waters cast,
Sink warrior-like to rest at last.

XVIII.

And he who stands as then I stood
By INCA-PAH-CO's glorious water,
And gazes on the haunted flood
Where long ago KACHESCO wooed
In early youth its Island daughter,
And threads that island's solitude,
Once witness of his loved one's slaughter,
At that same season of the leaf
In which I heard him tell his grief,

Will own 'mid autumn's wildest glory,
The wilder tissue of that story,
And feel—while shuddering at the view
Which, with each feature stern and true
Of his relentless race he drew—
Feel not yet wholly waste the mind
Where Faith so deep a root could find:
Faith which both love and life could save,
  And keep the first, in age still fond,
Yet blossoming this side the grave,
  In fadeless trust of fruit beyond!

XIX.

Long years had passed when I thus gazed,
By INCA-PAH-CO's beauty dazed;
Long years and many a distant scene
Of tamer life had come between,
Since by that nameless mountain tarn
  I realized, a stripling stout,
  My first night's fun of "camping out,"
And listened to the Indian yarn
  I here am going to tell about;
Whose wampum beads, perchance astray,
Had idly slipped, unstrung, away—
Save now in coasting that bright shore
    Where INCA-PAH-CO's wavelets chime.
The sounds that moved my soul of yore,
  The scene of our lone bivouac
  Came, each and all, as freshly back,
    Beneath the crisp October prime,

As springs by matted leaves choked up
Which brighten in the hoof-stamped cup,
  Upon the Caribou's wild track.

XX.

Again KACHESCO's face of truth
  I saw before my fancy move,
Fixed as the memory of my youth,
  And sad as all it knew of love.
  Again, as chiller blew the blast,
When he had ceased to speak that night—
  While I, still wakeful, pondered o'er
  His wondrous story more and more—
I saw him moving in the light
  The fire which he was feeding cast;
Again his words were in my ear,
As I'll repeat them simply here,
  And tell the tale from first to last.

XXI.

"I like Lake INCA-PAH-CO well,"
    Half mused aloud my wild-wood friend;
"Why, white man, I can hardly tell!
    For fish and deer, at either end,
  The rifts are good; but run-ways more
  There are by crooked KILLOQUORE
And RACQUET at the time of spearing,
    As well as that for yarding moose,
    Hath both enough for hunter's use:
Amid these hills are lakes appearing

More limpid to the Summer's eye;
In some at night the stars will twinkle
As if they dropp'd there from the sky
The pebbled bed below to sprinkle;
I ply my paddle in them all—
Of all, at times, a home have made—
Yet, stranger, when I've thither stray'd
I seem'd to hear the ripples fall
Each time still sweeter than before
On INCA-PAH-CO's winding shore."

XXII.

There was a sadness in his tone
His careless words would fain disown;
Or rather I would say their touch
Of mournfulness betray'd that much,
Much more of deep and earnest feeling
Was through his wither'd bosom stealing:
For now far back in memory
So much absorb'd he seem'd to be,
I'd not molest his revery;
And when—in phrase I now forget—
When I at last the silence broke,
In the same train of musing yet,
Watching awhile the wreathed smoke
Curl from his lighted calumet,
He thus aloud half pondering spoke:

XXIII.

"Years, years ago, when life was new,
And long before there was a clearing

Among these ADIRONDAC HIGHLANDS,
My sachem kept his best canoe
On one of INCA-PAH-CO's islands—
The largest which lies tow'rd the north,
As you are through the Narrows veering—
And there had reared his wigwam too.

"A trapper now, with years o'erladen,
He lived there with one only daughter,
A gentle but still gamesome maiden,
Who, I have heard, would venture forth,
Venture upon the darkest night
Across the broad and gusty water
To climb that cliff upon the main,
By some since call'd THE MAIDEN'S REST,
That foot save hers hath never press'd,
And watch the camp-fire's distant light,
Which told that she should see again
Her hunter when the dawn was bright."

XXIV.

He paused—look'd down, then stirr'd the fire,
He smiled—I did not like that smile,
As leaning on his elbow nigher
His bright eyes glared in mine the while,
And I was glad that scrutiny o'er,
When neither had misgivings more,
While he, in earnest now at last,
Reveal'd his memories of the past.

XXV.

"White man, thy look is open, kind,
    Thou scornest not a tale of truth!
Should I in thee a mocker find,
    'Twould shame alike thy blood and youth.
I trust thee! well, now look upon
    This wither'd cheek and shrunken form!
Canst think, young man, *I* was the one
    For whom that maiden dared the storm?
  Yes, often, till a tribesman came—
  It matters not to speak his name—
  A youth as tall, as straight, as I,
  As quick his quarry to descry,
  A hunter bold upon his prey
  As ever struck the elk at bay.
  —But thou shalt see him, if thou wilt
  Gaze on the wreck since made by guilt,—
Where glints its crag-drip to the moon,
And raves through soaking moss the Scroon,
To where Peseco's waters lave
  Its shining strand and beach-clad hills,
From hoarse Ausable's caverned wave
  To Saranac's most northern rills—
These woods around, do they not know
That doomed one's guilt, my sleepless woe?
  Know it in every glen and glade
  Of Adirondac's haunted shade,
Where branches bend or waters flow!

XXVI.

"Oft in that barren hollow, where
Through moss-hung hemlocks blasted, there

Whirl the dark rapids of Yowhayle;
Oft, too, by Teoratie blue,
And where the silent wave that slides
Tessuya's cedar islets through,
Cahogaronta's cliff divides
In foam through deep Kurloonah's vale—
Where great Tahawus splits the sky,
Where Borrhas greets his melting snows,
By those linked lakes that shining lie
Where Metauk's whispering forest grows—
From Nessingh's sluggish waters, red
With alder roots that line their bed,
To where, through many a grassy *vlie*,
The winding Atatea flows;
And from Oukorla's glistening eye
To hoary Wahopartenie,
As still from spot to spot we fled,
How often his despairing sigh,
How oft his hoarse, half-muttered cry
The very air has thickened
On which his fruitless prayer was sped!
Where naked Ounowarlah towers;
Where Sandanona's shadows float;
Where wind-swept Nodoneyo lowers,
And in that gorge's quaking throat,
Reft by OTNEYARH's giant band,
Where splinters of the mountain vast,
Though lashed by cable roots, aghast,
Toppling amid their ruin, stand;
Through Reuna's hundred isles of green,
By Onegora's pebbly pools;

Where Paskungamah's birches lean,
And where, through many a dark ravine,
The triple crown of crags is seen
By which grim Towaloondah rules—
By Gwi-endauqua's bristling fall,
Through Twen-ungasko's echoing glen,
To wild Ouluska's inmost den,
Alone—alone with that poor thrall,
I wrestled life away in all!"

XXVII.

Breathless, he paused, while vaguely stirred
By theme, as yet, all dark to me,
I thrilled beneath each savage word
That from his throat came savagely.
But now some softer memories make
That tawny bosom heave and swell,
As, gazing far into the night,
He rivets there his aching sight,
Nor will again his tale forsake,
Till there's no more to tell.

PART II.—THE VIGIL OF FAITH.

I.

"BRIGHT NULKAH, doe-eyed forest girl!
Oh! still in dreams those evening skies
Bend over me as soft as when,
Born to a faith first plighted then,
We silent sought each other's eyes
To read their spirit mysteries:
Then watched the lake's low ripples curl,

Then sought each other's eyes again,
Then looked around on crag and hill,
Looked on each shadowy tree so still,
Looked on them each and all to see
All—all was *real,* Earth—Love and WE.

II.

"I round her neck the wampum threw,
String after string she kissed them each,
And parting at the water's edge
When I had launched my light canoe,
Unwilling yet to leave the beach,
But poised upon a fallen tree
I long could see the holy pledge,
Pressed to her heart or waved to me:
Could see it glimmer in the dew
Yet—yet again from rocky ledge,
When, after the first head-land cast
My boat in shadow as I pass'd,
Again across the moonlit bay,
She saw my glistening paddle play
And gave me back one answering ray.

III.

"Ah! bounding then the broad lake over,
What vigor to my arm love gave!
What life, fresh life to every wave,
That buoy'd up my NULKAH'S lover!
And sadly as she left me there,
How much of sweetness was to spare
For her who soon would climb the cliff,
To vainly watch my coming skiff,

Would toiling gain the rugged height,
  To suffer all love's sadness where
It came unmixed with love's delight
  And seemed the herald of Despair!

IV.

"I sent to her—I sent a friend,
  The chosen one of all our band,
With whom my heart was wont to blend
  Like those which mate in spirit land.
From SACANDAOA's fountain head
  Where in our camp I fevered lay,
Through NUSHIONA's vale he sped,
  And gained her home at close of day.
Beside her father's fire he slept—
  It was too late to speak that night,
And when my NULKAH's beauty first
Upon him with the morning burst,
  He had no tongue to speak aright,
And still my message from her kept—
  Kept back love's message day by day
  Till sullen weeks had worn away,
While lonely NULKAH often wept.

V.

"Nay, more, when she would cross the wave
    At midnight in the wildest weather,
While tempests round the peak would rave
    From which she watch'd for nights together,

He told—that tribesman whom I loved,
Yes, loved as if he were my brother—
He told her that the woods I roved
To feed the lodge where dwelt another:
Another who now cherish'd there
The child that claim'd a hunter's care;
Claim'd it upon some distant shore,
From which I would return no more.

VI.

"All this in her had wrought no change,
No anxious doubt, no jealous fear,
But he, meanwhile, had words most strange
Breathed in my gentle NULKAH's ear,
Which made her wish that I were near:
Words strange to her, who, simple, true,
And only love as prosperous knew,
Shrank from the fitful fantasy,
Which, seeming less like love than hate,
Would cloud his moody brow when he,
Gazing on her, arraigned the fate
Which could such loveliness create
Only to work him misery.
And when she heard that lying tale,
Her woman's heart could soon discover
Some double treachery might assail,
Through him, her unsuspecting lover;
And Love in fear, still fearless, brought her
On errand Love in hope first taught her.

VII.

"I came at last. She ask'd me naught—
It was enough to see me there;
But of the friend who thus had wrought,
Though he now streams far distant sought,
She bade me in the wood beware.
A wound my coming had delay'd,
And still too weak to use my gun,
I set the nets the old chief made;
Baited his traps in forest glade;
And sweetly after woo'd the maid,
At evening when my toils were done.

VIII.

"'Twas then I chose a grassy swale,
In which my wigwam frame to make;
Shelter'd by crags from northern gale,
Shaded by boughs, save toward the lake.
The RED-BIRD's nest above it swung;
There often the MA-MA-TWA sung;
And MONING-GWUNA's quills of gold
Through leaves like flickering sunshine told;
There, too, when Spring was backward, first,
Her shrinking blossoms safely burst;
And there, when autumn leaf was sere,
Some flowers still stay'd the loitering year.

IX.

"She learn'd full soon to love the spot,
For who could see and love it not?

Why, Morning there had newer splendor,
There, Twilight seemed to grow more tender,
And Moonbeams first would thither stray,
To light PUCKWUDJEES to their play.
And there, when I the isle would leave,
And sometimes now my gun resume,
She'd shyly steal the mats to weave
Which were to line our bridal room.
Happy we were! what love like ours,
Blossoming thus as fresh and free,
As unrestrain'd as wild-wood flowers,
Yet keeping all their purity!

X.

"Happy we were! my secret foe,
How dread a foe, I knew not then,
Remain'd to fish the streams below
That into CADARAQUI flow,
Returning to us only when
Some kinsmen on our bridal morn,
Impell'd by a mysterious doom
Which with that fateful man was born,
Brought him to shroud the day in gloom
And blast our joys about to bloom.

XI.

"Just MANITOU! Oh may the boat
That bears him to the spirit land
For ages on those black waves float
Which catch no light from off its strand,

Float blindly there, still laboring on
Toward shores 'tis never doom'd to reach;
Float there till time itself is gone,
And when again 'twould seek the beach
From which with that lone soul it started,
Baffling let *that* before it flee,
Till hope of rest hath all departed,
And still when that last hope is gone,
A guideless thing, float on, float on!

XII.

"The birds of song had sunk to rest;
The eagle's tireless wing was furl'd;
On INCA-PAH-CO's darkening breast
The last few golden ripples curl'd:
The distant mountains, bright before,
Now seem'd to darken more and more
Against the eastern sky;
Until a white pine's slender cone,
Tapering above the hill-top, shone,
And show'd the moon was nigh.
Our friends, they all stood gravely round,
Waiting until that moon should rise,
The bridal moon whose aspect crown'd,
For good or ill, our destinies:
The signal too, the hour had come,
When I could claim my bride and home.

XIII.

"Blushing at that fast-brightening sky,
When on her father's lodge it shone,

How did she shrink within, when I
Would lead that loved one to my own!
Forth stepp'd e'en then that dismal guest
Who grimly stood amid the rest,
And, while his knife he drew,
With cry that made us all aghast,
And frantic gesture, hurrying past,
He sprang the threshold through.

XIV.

"A shriek! and I with soul of flame
Devour'd the fearful space between:
Another and another came
E'en while my grip was on his throat,
Where, writhing in the dark unseen,
His victim in her gore did float!
And life was oozing through each wound
That gash'd her lovely form about,
When, hurling him upon the ground,
I bore her to the light without.

XV.

"Aided by that untimely beam,
Which harbinger'd such bridal woes,
I watch'd its ebbing current gleam,
And, watching, would not, could not, deem
That blessed life's too precious stream
Growing each moment darker, colder,
E'en while I to my heart did fold her,
Already at its close.

She tried to speak—then press'd my hand,
And look'd—oh, look'd into my eyes
As if through them the spirit land
Would first upon her vision rise:
As if her soul, that could not stay,
Through mine might only pass away.

XVI.

"I know not when that look did fade,
Nor when did fail that dying grasp,
Nor how they loosed the lifeless maid,
Stiffening within love's desperate clasp.
The sod upon her grave was green,
The leaflet greening on the oak,
The autumn and the winter o'er,
When I once more to sense awoke,—
Awoke to know some joys had been
Which now to me could be no more;
Awoke to know that life to me
Was henceforth but a *girdled* tree
Whose tough limbs still must bide the blast
Until the trunk to earth be cast,
Though fruit nor blossom ne'er can smile
Upon those wrestling limbs the while.

XVII.

"He still was there, that youth accurst,
Who thus through blood his end had sought,
He who, with frenzied love athirst,
Such wreck of loveliness had wrought.

He still was there, for while I breathed,
With sense and feeling almost gone—
The aged father, thus bereaved,
Raving the wretch should still live on—
Of all our friends there was not one
Would deal the vengeance they believed
'Twas mine on him to wreak alone.

XVIII.

"He still was there. 'Twas he that kept
A nurse's watch while thus I slept:
Ever and ever by my side,
With anxious eye and noiseless tread,
Hanging about my fever'd bed,
With none he would his task divide:
Trembling, with jealous fear afraid,
When near the grave I seem'd to hover,
Lest that bright land which claim'd the maid
Was opening too upon her lover.

XIX.

"And now, when, no more languishing,
My mind and strength became renew'd,
Amid the balmy airs of spring,
And I once more could take the wood;
Think you he fear'd the bloody fate
Which blood will alway expiate?
Oh no! he look'd too far before—
Look'd far beyond this fleeting shore,
Where bliss will die as soon as born!

He hoped, he blindly trusted, he,
That on the instant that I woke
Revenge would be so fierce in me,
I'd madly deal some deathful stroke,
Would send his soul where hers was gone!

XX.

"But I—I knew too well his guile,
'Twas whisper'd me in dreams the while,
I saw a form about my bed,
That alway shrunk from him with dread:
'Twould come by night, 'twould come by day,
But clearest in the moonbeam show,
Then ever, as it nearer drew
Ere melting from my wistful view,
With palm reversed, it seem'd to say,
'If yet thou wilt not with me go,
Keep him—*oh keep but him away!*'

XXI.

"And did I not? ay, while the knell
Of youth and hope yet echo'd by,
Did I not then allay thy fears,
Perturbed soul, that his was nigh?
And o'er the waste of dreary years,
On which, heart-wither'd, doom'd to dwell,
I look with weary vision back—
Have I not on that desert track,
Sweet spirit, kept love's vigil well?
Oh have I not? Yes—though no more
I see at night those moon-touch'd fingers,
Still beckoning as they did of yore;

And though the features of my love,
As near me still in dreams she lingers,
Look bright, as yon bright star above,
And peaceful, as in that blest time,
When our young loves were in their prime—
I know that from the land of shades,
When wandering thus to haunt these glades,
The vigil to her soul is dear
I kept, and still am keeping here!
—Enough of this, thou still wouldst know
How dealt I with my mortal foe.

XXII.

"The stag that snuffs the breeze of morn
Where first it lifts the birchen spray,
Gazing on lakes all newly born
From valley mists that roll away,
Treads not the upland fern more free,
Looks not with eye more bright below,
Than moved and look'd that man, when he
Strode forth and stood beneath the tree
To bide my avenging hatchet's blow:
The crestless doe, whose faint limbs sink
Beside the rill to which they bore her—
Life-stricken on its very brink
That instant when she'd gasping drink
From the bright wave that leaps before her—
Lies not more lowly and forlorn,
All stretch'd upon the forest leaves,
Than near the tree that Outcast lay,
When, by my gleaming hatchet shorn,

His warrior-tuft is cleft away,
And he the living doom receives
To wander thus where'er he may—
Of woman and of man the scorn!

XXIII.

"A month went by; the wigwam-smoke
No more from that cold hearth ascended,
Where the old chief no longer woke
To woes that with his life were ended:
A month, and that deserted isle
Was left alone to me and *her!*
The summer had begun to smile,
The winds of June the leaves to stir;
And flowers that budded late the while,
To bloom above her sepulchre;
Meek, pallid things, grave-nursed below,
That feebly there as yet would grow,
Brighter in coming years to blow—
And where was he whose fell despair
The Flower of Love laid bleeding there?

XXIV.

"Shooting from out the leafy land,
Right opposite our island home,
There was a narrow neck of sand,
O'er which the wave on either hand
Would fling at times its crest of foam.
And here—as I one morning stood
Upon a rock which faced that beach—
I saw, wild rushing from the wood,
Within my loaded rifle's reach,

A figure that distracted ran
Until it gain'd the frothy marge,
And there an unarm'd, kneeling man
Bared his broad bosom to my charge!

XIV.

"I stood, but did not raise the gun—
Although it rattled in my grasp—
I stood and coldly look'd upon
The suppliant, who still lower bent,
His hands in agony did clasp,
As if the soul within him pent
Would rend its penal tenement.
At last, with low half smother'd cry
And quivering frame, he gain'd his feet,
And to the woods began to fly,
Growing at every step more fleet:
But from that hour, where'er he fled,
There too my shadow darkened!

XXVI.

"One moment was enough to bind
Firmly my weapons on my head,
The strait was swum, and far behind
The crested waves effaced my tread
Upon the beach, o'er which I sped
So swiftly that the forest glade
At once the wanderer's trail betray'd;
And though it led o'er rocky ledge,
Led oft within the pool's black edge,
'Twas soon reveal'd anew—

The springy moss just crisping back
I saw upon his recent track,
Nor paused to trace it in the brook,
Whose alders still behind him shook
Where he had bounded through.

XXVII.

"And—when again the stream he cross'd,
Where, in its forks, awhile I lost
His trail amid the maze
Of severing rills, and run-ways wound
About the deer lick's trampled ground—
The very living things around,
Which in these forest-depths abound,
The sable darting from the fern,
The gliding ermine, each in turn,
His whereabout betrays;
From plunging beaver's warning stroke,
From wood-duck whirring from the oak,
And screaming loon, alike I learn
Where lead the wanderer's ways.

XXVIII.

"At length within a broken dell,
Where a gnarl'd beech the tempest shock
Had parted from the leaning rock,
Among its cable roots, he fell;
Where, panting, soon I saw him lie,
Shrivelling against the blasted trunk,
With knees drawn up and cowering eye,
As if my avenging tread had shrunk
The miscreant there as I drew nigh.

I spoke not—but I gazed upon
That wolf with fangs and courage gone,
Gazed on his quailing features till
Their furtive glance was fix'd by mine,
And I could see his writhing will
Her feeble throne to me resign.

XXIX.

"He rose, an abject, broken man,
He dared not fight—he dared not fly;
His very life in my veins ran,
Who would not let him cast it by!
And still he is the thing that then
He wilted to within that glen:
Living—if life be drawing breath—
But dead in all that last should die,
For him there is no further death
Till from the earth he withereth.

XXX.

"I hunt for him—I dress his food,
I guide his footsteps in the wood,
Or, when alone for game I'd beat,
Direct where we at night shall meet.
He cleans my arms—my snow-shoes makes;
He bales my shallop on the lakes;
And when with fishing spear I glide
At midnight o'er the silent tide,
'Tis he who holds the pine-knot torch,
That seems her blazing path to scorch
Where waves o'er reddening shoals divide.

XXXI.

"With me he now is alway meek,
    But sometimes, chafing in his thrall,
He to my dog will sharply speak,
    Who comes, or comes not at his call.
They both are in my camp below,
    From which I now in hunting weather
For days can often safely go,
    Leaving the two alone together.
But in those years my watch began
    His limbs were agile as my own,
And sometimes then the tortured man
    For weeks beyond my search hath flown,
    In shades more deep to breathe alone.

XXXII.

"But ever when he thus would flee,
Flee from himself as well as me,
Some hollow trunk or swampy lair
Betrayed his howlings of despair,
As near the she-wolf ceased her moan
To listen to his dreaming groan,
Or, scared from perch on dead branch by,
The fish-hawk caught his sharper cry,
When light that waked from seeming pain
Brought back the living sense again.
And sometimes then with strange dismay,
    Flinging a frantic look around,
He from the "windfall's" ghastly fray
    Of uptorn trunks would shrieking bound,

As if from their convulsion grew
Some shape to his distracted view,
Some hideous shape his soul first caught
From havoc there by Nature wrought!
Then shivering in each limb with dread,
As o'er the quaking bog he fled,
And, flying toward it, still afraid
To reach again the forest shade,
He joyed that even I was near
To soothe him in his mortal fear.

XXXIII.

"Again, when in his wildest mood,
He would some mystic power obey,
Which from that island's haunted wood
Ne'er let him wander far away,
And alway soon or late I could
Steal on him in his solitude:
While oft, as weaker grew his brain,
And he forgot God's law of blood,
I've track'd the poor bewilder'd thing,
Wherever he was famishing;
And snatched him o'er and o'er again
From death he sought by fell and flood.

XXXIV.

"Sometimes, when wintry snows were deep,
And game was scarce within our range,
When near our camp 'twere death to keep,
Yet lacked we strength our camp to change:

Compell'd, in search of food, to creep
  Through smothering drift and snowy surge,
We'd starving sink in snow to sleep,
  Through sleet the morrow to emerge—
My arms around him I would bind,
To shield him from the wintry wind,
And still his hand close clutching, hold
  When through the morrow's whirling blast
Our languid steps were tottering told,
  Where ice some dizzy ledge had glass'd,
And reeling 'neath the tempest's breath,
Our pinch'd-up limbs trod near to death.
Then, lest his soul should slip away
That night from his half-torpid clay,
    I'd warm against my breast his feet,
    And constant wake to feel if heat
    Of life still in his pulses beat.

XXXV.

"And when spring thaws dissolved the snow,
  And, loosened from their ancient stay,
In mass, dissevered at a blow,
Old trees and root-inwoven ground
With rocks and ice together bound,
  Would plunging crash their headlong way,
And scatter waste and ruin wide
Far down the mountain's riven side—
As then our wild-wood track would go
Across the swollen torrent's flow,

Often, ere this, my frail canoe
  Upon the freshet's foam has toss'd,
Where splintered ice would thunder through
  The roaring gulf which I have crossed
To bridge for him the tide below.
And ever then my voice has lent
  Fresh vigor to his trembling knee,
As shrinking he before me went,
Appalled to hear the surges hiss
  So close beneath the slippery tree,
That tottering spanned the dread abyss.

XXXVI.

"When summer drought has parched the ground,
And crisped the dusty leaves around,
    Encircled by the forest fire,
And gasping in its blinding smoke,
    My bleeding way through walls of brier,
Half stifled, I have desperate broke,
  And dragged him to some lonely peak,
Where o'er his prostrate form I stood,
  And watched the Flaming Spirit wreak
    His wrath each moment nigher—nigher—
Have watched him whirling through the wood,
    Resistless in each angry coil,
  Now scorching up the brush beneath,
    Shrivelling alike both root and soil,
  Now fastening on some hoary pine,
    And vomiting his burning breath
  On writhing limbs through which he'd twine—

Darting aloft his crimson tongue
The sharply crackling boughs among,
Until the crag round which he swept,
The crag where our last hold we kept,
One blazing pyre of light became,
An islet in a sea of flame.
There, bending oft that faint wretch over—
His body with my own to cover—
There, while the moss whereon he lay
In blistered flakes would peel away,
Between him and the flames I cast
My form, until the peril passed.

XXXVII.

"And thus as crowding seasons changed,
  When many a year was dead and gone,
I round these lakes in manhood ranged,
  Where yet in age I wander on,
    And still o'er that poor slave I've kept
    A vigil that hath never slept;
And while upon this earth I stay,
From her I'll still keep him away—
From her whom I at last shall see
My own, my own eternally!

XXXVIII.

"White man! I say not that they lie
    Who preach a faith so dark and drear
That wedded hearts in yon cold sky
    Meet not as they were mated here.

But scorning not thy faith, thou must,
Stranger, in mine have equal trust:
The Red man's faith by Him implanted,
Who souls to both our races granted.
Thou know'st in life we mingle not,
Death cannot change our different lot!
He who hath placed the White man's heaven
Where hymns on vapory clouds are chanted,
To harps by angel fingers play'd;
Not less on his Red children smiles
To whom a land of souls is given,
Where in the ruddy west array'd
Brighten our blessed hunting isles.

XXXIX.

"There souls again to youth are born,
A youth that knows no withering!
There, blithe and bland, the breeze of morn
Fresheneth an eternal Spring
'Mid trees, and flowers, and waterfalls,
And fountains bubbling from the moss,
And leaves that quiver with delight,
As from their shade the warbler calls,
Or choiring, glances to the light
On wings which never lose their gloss:
There brooks that bear their buds away,
From branches that will bend above them,
So closely they could not but love them,
To the same bowers again will stray
From which at first they murmuring sever,

Still floating back their blossoms to them,
Still with the same sweet music ever,
Returning yet once more to woo them;
There love, like bird and brook and blossom,
Is young for ever in each bosom!

XL.

"Those blissful ISLANDS OF THE WEST:
I've seen, myself, at sunset time,
The golden lake in which they rest;
Seen too, the barks that bear The Blest
Floating toward that fadeless clime:
First dark, just as they leave our shore,
Their sides then brightening more and more,
Till in a flood of crimson light
They melted from my straining sight.
And she, who climb'd the storm-swept steep,
She who the foaming wave would dare,
So oft love's vigil here to keep,
Stranger, albeit thou think'st I dote,
I know, I know she watches there!
Watches upon that radiant strand,
Watches to see her lover's boat
Approach The Spirit-Land."

Rhymes on West Point.

I'VE trod thy mountain paths, thy valleys deep,
Through mazy thickets, and through tangled heath;
I've climb'd thy piled up rocks, from steep to steep,
And gazed with rapture on the scene beneath.

The noble plain that lies embosom'd there,
The jutting headlands in thy mimic bay—
The stream, impatient of his curb'd career,
Sweeping through mighty mountains far away,

His bosom burnish'd by the setting sun,
Who, loath to leave his own illumined west,
Dyes with his hues the waves he shines upon,
And gilds the clouds which cradle him to rest.

I love West Point, and long could fondly dwell
On scenes which must through life my memory haunt,
But you, too, reader, have been there as well
As I—if not, you'd better take the jaunt.

You rise at six and by half after ten
You're at the Point—I was when last I went—
You rest awhile at Cozzens's, and then
May stroll toward the upper Monument.

At two you dine (you'll think it not too soon,
Being sharp set from your long morning's ramble),

And to Fort Putnam in the afternoon,
O'er rocks and brushwood up the mountain scramble.

The view which this majestic height commands
Repays the trouble of its rough access;
For he beholds, who on the rampart stands,
A scene of grandeur and of loveliness:

The chain of mountains, sweeping far away—
The white encampment spread beneath his feet—
The sloop, slow dropping down the placid bay,
Her form reflected in its glassy sheet.

And where the river's banks less boldly swell,
Villas upon some sunny slope are seen;
And white huts buried in some wooded dell,
With chimneys peering through their leafy screen.

'Tis sweet to watch from hence at close of day,
While shadows lengthen on the mountain side,
The sunbeams steal from peak to peak away,
And white sails gleam along the dusky tide.

And sweet to woman's eye, at evening hour,
The gay parade that animates the plain,
When martial music lends its kindling power,
To thrill the bosom with some stirring strain—

Who, when they to their gleaming ranks repair,
Delight to gaze upon the bright array

Of young, good-looking fellows marshall'd there
  In pigeon-breasted coats of iron-gray.

For girls the glare of warlike pomp adore,
  Since, cased in steel, with lance and curtle-axe on,
Bold Cœur-de-Lion led his knights to war,
  Down to the days of Major-General Jackson.

At night, when home returning, it is sweet,
  While stars are twinkling in the fields above,
And whispering breezes in the foliage meet,
  To move in such a scene with one we love.

To feel the spell of woman's witchery near,
  And while the magic o'er our senses steals,
Believe the being whom we hold most dear,
  As deeply as ourselves that moment feels.

* * * * * * *

The dolphin's hues are brightest while he dies,
  The rainbow's glories in their birth decay,
And love's bright visions, like our autumn skies,
  Will fade the soonest when they seem most gay.

In "true love" now I am an arrant skeptic,
  My heart's best music is for ever hush'd;
Perhaps because I'm briefless and dyspeptic,
  Perhaps my hopes were once too rudely crush'd.

But to return—to lawyerling too poor,
  Leaving his duns and office to a friend,
To take the northern or the eastern tour,
  This short excursion I will recommend.

'Tis but two dollars and a day bestow'd,
  And far from town, its dust and busy strife,
You'll find the jaunt a pleasing episode
  In the dull epic of a city life.

THE FOREST CEMETERY.

I.

WILD Tawasentha !* in thy brook-laced glen
  The doe no longer lists her lost fawn's bleating,
As panting there, escaped from hunter's ken,
  She hears the chase o'er distant hills retreating ;
No more, uprising from the fern around her,
  The Indian archer, from his "still-hunt" lair,
Wings the death-shaft which hath that moment found her
  When Fate seemed foiled upon her footsteps there :

II.

Wild Tawasentha ! on thy cone-strew'd sod,
  O'er which yon Pine his giant arm is bending,
No more the Mohawk marks its dark crown nod
  Against the sun's broad disk toward night descending ;

* Tawasentha, meaning in Mohawk "The place of the many dead," is the finely appropriate name of the new Forest Cemetery on the banks of the Hudson, between Albany and Troy.

Then crouching down beside the brands that redden
The columned trunks which rear thy leafy dome,
Forgets his toils in hunter's slumbers leaden,
Or visions of the Red Man's spirit home:

III.

But where his calumet by that lone fire,
At night beneath these cloister'd boughs was lighted,
The Christian orphan will in prayer aspire,
The Christian parent mourn his proud hope blighted;
And in thy shade the mother's heart will listen
The spirit-cry of babe she clasps no more,
And where thy rills through hemlock branches glisten,
There many a maid her lover will deplore.

IV.

Here children linked in love and sport together,
Who check their mirth as creaks the slow hearse by,
Will totter lonely in life's autumn weather,
To ponder where life's springtime blossoms lie;
And where the virgin soil was never dinted
By the rude ploughshare since creation's birth,
Year after year fresh furrows will be printed
Upon the sad cheek of the grieving earth.

V.

Yon sun, returning in unwearied stages,
Will gild the cenotaph's ascending spire

O'er names on history's yet unwritten pages
  That unborn crowds will, worshipping, admire ;
Names that shall brighten through my country's story
  Like meteor hues that fire her autumn woods,
Encircling high her onward course of glory
  Like the bright bow which spans her mountain
    floods.

VI.

Here where the flowers had bloomed and died for
    ages—
  Bloomed all unseen and perished all unsung—
On youth's green grave, traced out beside the sage's,
  Will garlands now by votive hearts be flung ;
And sculptured marble and funereal urn,
  O'er which gray birches to the night air wave,
Will whiten through thy glades at every turn,
  And woo the moonbeam to some poet's grave !

VII.

Thus back to Nature, faithful, do we come,
  When Art hath taught us all her best beguiling—
Thus blend their ministry around the tomb
  Where pointing upward still sits Nature smiling !
And never, Nature's hallowed spots adorning,
  Hath Art with her a sombre garden dress'd,
Wild Tawasentha ! in this vale of mourning,
  With more to consecrate their children's rest.

VIII.

And still that stream will hold its winsome way,
  Sparkling as now upon the frosty air,
When all in turn shall troop in pale array
  To that dim land for which so few prepare.
Still will yon oak which now a sapling waves,
  Each year renewed, with hardy vigor grow,
Expanding still to shade the nameless graves
  Of nameless men that haply sleep below.

IX.

Nameless as they,—in one dear memory blest,
  How tranquil in these phantom peopled bowers
Could I here wait the partner of my rest
  In some green nook, that should be only ours:
Under old boughs, where moist the livelong summer
  The moss is green and springy to the tread,
Where thou, my friend, shouldst be an often comer
  To pierce the thicket, seeking for my bed:

X.

For thickets heavy all around should screen it
  From careless gazer that might wander near,
Nor e'en to him who by some chance had seen it
  Would I have aught to catch his eye appear:
One lonely stem—a trunk those old boughs lifting,
  Should mark the spot; and, haply, new thrift owe
To that which upward through its sap was drifting
  From what lay mouldering round its roots below.

XI.

The Wood-duck there her glossy-throated brood
Should unmolested gather to her wings;
The schoolboy, awed, as near that mound he stood,
Should spare the Redstart's nest that o'er it swings,
And thrill, when there, to hear the cadenc'd winding
Of boatman's horn upon the distant river,
Dell unto dell in long-link'd echoes binding—
Like far-off requiem, floating on for ever.

XII.

There my freed spirit with the dawn's first beaming
Would come to revel round the dancing spray;
There would it linger with the day's last gleaming,
To watch thy footsteps thither track their way.
The quivering leaf should whisper in that hour
Things that for thee alone would have a sound,
And parting boughs my spirit-glances shower
In gleams of light upon the mossy ground.

XIII.

There, when long years and all thy journeyings over,
Loosed from this world thyself to join the free,
Thou too wouldst come to rest beside thy lover
In that sweet cell beneath our Trysting-Tree;
Where earliest birds above our narrow dwelling
Should pipe their matins as the morning rose,
And woodland symphonies majestic swelling,
In midnight anthem, hallow our repose.

Love Poems.

LOVE POEMS.

LOVE'S CALENDAR; OR, EROS AND ANTEROS.

LOVE, with the ancient sages, if it be not twin-born, yet hath a brother wondrous like him, called Anteros; whom while he seeks all about, his chance is to meet with many false and feigning desires that wander singly up and down in his likeness. By them, in their borrowed garb, is Love often deceived; partly that his eye is not the quickest in this dark region here below (which is not love's proper sphere), partly out of the simplicity and credulity which is native to him, and embraces and consorts him with those suborned striplings, as if they were his mother's own sons. But after awhile, soaring above the shadow of the earth, he discerns that this is not his genuine brother, as he imagined; he has no longer the power to hold fellowship with such a personate mate. For that original and fiery virtue given him, by fate, all on a sudden goes out, and leaves him undeified and despoiled of all his force; till finding Anteros at last, he kindles and repairs the almost faded ammunition of his deity, by the reflection of a coequal and homogeneal fire.—MILTON.

I.

THEY are mockery all—those skies, those skies—
Their untroubled depths of blue;
They are mockery all—these eyes, these eyes,
Which seem so warm and true.

Each quiet star in the one that lies,
Each meteor glance that at random dies
  The other's lashes through;
They are mockery all, these flowers of spring,
  Which her airs so softly woo;
And the love to which we would madly cling,
  Ay! it is mockery too;
The winds are false which the perfume stir,
  And the looks deceive to which we sue,
And love but leads to the sepulchre,
  Which the flowers spring to strew.

II.

Ay! there it is, that winning smile,
  That look that cheats my heart for ever,
That tone that will my brain beguile
  Till reason from her seat shall sever.
All, all bewitching, as when last
  I for the twentieth time forswore them,
Resistless as when first I cast
  My whole adoring soul before them.

Like carrier doves that hurry back
  To the bright home from which they're parted,
However blind may be their track,
  Or far the goal from which they started,—
So from Love's jesses if e'er free
  I set my thoughts one moment roving,
Somehow the very next in thee
  They always find their home of loving.

III.

She loves—but 'tis not me she loves :—
  Not me on whom she ponders,
When in some dream of tenderness
  Her truant fancy wanders.
The forms that flit her visions through
  Are like the shapes of old,
Where tales of Prince and Paladin
  On tapestry are told.
Man may not hope her heart to win,
  Be his of common mould !

But I—though spurs are won no more
  Where herald's trump is pealing,
Nor thrones carved out for lady fair
  Where steel-clad ranks are wheeling—
I loose the falcon of my hopes
  Upon as proud a flight
As they who hawk'd at high renown,
  In song-ennobled fight.
If *daring* then true love may crown,
  My love she must requite !

IV.

Tell her I love her—love her for those eyes
  Now soft with feeling, radiant now with mirth,
Which, like a lake reflecting autumn skies,
  Reveal two heavens here to us on earth—
The one in which their soulful beauty lies,
  And that wherein such soulfulness has birth :
Go, autumn flower, before the season flies,

And the rude winter comes thy bloom to blast—
Go! and with all of eloquence thou hast,
  The burning story of my love discover,
  And if the theme should fail, alas! to move her,
Tell her, when youth's gay budding time is past,
  And summer's gaudy flowering is over,
Like thee, my love will blossom to the last!

V.

Her heart is like a harp whose strings
  At will are touched alike by all:
Her heart is like a bird that sings
  In answer to each fowler's call.
That harp!—has it one secret tone
Reserved for master hands alone?
That bird! has it one soulful note
Which only toward its mate will float?

Let it not wile thy soul away,
  That harp, with its beguiling touch;
Let not that bird's bewildering lay
  Thrill through thy bosom over-much:
They'll cheat thine eyes of sleep to-night,
Yet find thee dreaming with the light
With heart and brain all idly stirred—
The music of that harp and bird!

VI.

Tis hard to share her smiles with many!
  And while she is so dear to me,
To fear that I, far less than any,
  Call out her spirit's witchery!

To find my inmost heart when near her
  Trembling at every glance and tone,
And feel the while each charm grow dearer
  That will not beam for me alone.

How can she thus, sweet spendthrift, squander
  The treasures one alone can prize?
How can her eyes to all thus wander,
  When I but live in those sweet eyes?
Those syren tones so lightly spoken
  Cause many a heart I know to thrill;
But mine, and only mine, till broken,
  In every pulse must answer still.

VII.

Well! call it *Friendship!* have I asked for more,
Even in those moments when I gave the most?
'Twas but for thee I looked so far before!
I saw thy bark was hurrying blindly on,
A guideless thing upon a dangerous coast,—
With thee,—with thee, where would I not have gone?
But could I see thee *drift* upon the shore,
Unknowing drift, upon a shore unknown?
Yes, call it Friendship, and let no revealing,
If Love be there, e'er make Love's wild name heard,
It will not die, if it be worth concealing!
Call it then Friendship—but oh, let that word
Speak but for me—for me, a deeper feeling
Than ever yet a lover's bosom stirred!

VIII.

As he who, on some clouded night,
  When wind and tide attend his bark,
Waits for the North star's steady light
  To shine above the waters dark,
Will often for its guiding beam
  Mistake some wandering meteor's ray;
But wilder'd by that fitful gleam
Doubt yet to launch upon the stream,
  Till wind and tide have passed away,—

So I, if ever Life's dark sea
  Be swept by some propitious gale,
Look for my guiding light in thee,
  Before I dare to spread my sail;
So, while thy smiles deceitful shine,
  Then leave all darker than before,
I for some surer beacon pine,
Till, breeze and flood no longer mine,
  I'm stranded on the barren shore.

IX.

I will love her no more!—'tis a waste of the heart,
This lavish of feeling—a prodigal's part—
Who, heedless, the treasure a life could not earn
Squanders forth where he vainly may look for return.

I will love her no more—it is folly to give
Our best years to one, when for many we live.
And he who the world will thus barter for one,
I ween, by such traffic must soon be undone.

I will love her no more—it is heathenish thus
To bow to an idol which bends not to us;
Which heeds not, which hears not, which recks not
for aught
That the worship of years to its altar hath brought.

I will love her no more—for no love is without
Its limit in measure, and mine hath run out;
She engrosseth it all, and till some she restore,
Than this moment I love her—how can I love *more?*

X.

Oh! how could my heart so falsely gauge,
Singing that *more* than now I could not love thee!
Others, like me, may, at thy budding age,
Hold every feeling in sweet vassalage
Unto thy charms. But I—by all above me!—
Will prove thee suzerain of my soul more nearly;
When Time his arts shall 'gainst thy beauty wage,
To break their serfdom—serving thee more dearly.

Mark how the sunset, with its parting hues,
The heaving bosom of yon river staineth!
To yield those tints the grieving waves refuse,
Nor yet that purpling light at last will lose
Till Night itself, like Death, above them reigneth!
So *more* and *more* will brighten to the last
The light which, once upon my true soul cast,
Reflected there, still true till death remaineth.

XI.

Think not I love thee—by my word I do not!
Think not I love thee—for thy love I sue not!

And yet, I fear, there's hardly one that weareth
Thy beauty's chains, who like me for thee careth!
Who joys like me when in thy joy believing—
Who like me grieves when thou dost seem but griev-
ing?
But, though I charms so perilous eschew not,
Think not I love thee—trust me that I do not!

Think not I love thee!—pr'ythee why so coy, then?
Doth it thy maiden bashfulness annoy, then?
Sith the heart's homage still will be up-welling,
Where Truth and Goodness have so sweet a dwelling?
Surely, unjust one, I were less than mortal,
Knelt I not thus before that temple's portal.
Others dare to love thee—dare what I do not—
Then let me worship, bright one, while I woo not!

XII.

I know thou dost love me—ay! frown as thou wilt,
And curl that beautiful lip,
Which I never can gaze on without the guilt
Of burning its dew to sip:
I know that my heart is reflected in thine,
And, like flowers that over a brook incline,
They toward each other dip.

Though thou lookest so cold in these halls of light,
'Mid the careless, proud, and gay,
I will steal like a thief in thy heart at night,
And pilfer its thoughts away.

I will come in thy dreams at the midnight hour,
And thy soul in secret shall own the power
It dares to mock by day.

XIII.

I ask not what shadow came over her heart
In the moment I thought her my own—
If love in that moment could really depart,
I mourn not such love when 'tis flown.
I ask not what shadow came over her then,
What doubt did her bosom appal,
For I know where her heart will turn truly again,
If it ever turn truly at all!

It is not at once that the reed-bird takes wing,
When the tide rises high round her nest,
But again and again, floating back, she will sing
O'er the spot where her love-treasures rest:
And oh, when the surge of distrust would invade,
Where the heart hoped for ever to dwell,
Love long upon loitering pinion is stay'd,
Ere his wing waves a mournful farewell.

XIV.

I waited for thee—but all restless waited,
For soul like mine, it ever must be moving;
I knew one spirit with my own was mated,
Yet I mistook that restlessness for loving:
Of mine own nature an ideal created,
And loved because I only thus was fated.

Fated, bewilder'd thus in thought and feeling,
  To waste the freshness of my soul away,
To see each bud of spring in turn revealing
  But canker'd blooms upon a fruitless spray,—
Why marvel then in prayer I oft am kneeling,
Sweet minister of grace! to bless thy spirit-healing?

XV.

My life's whole pilgrimage have I not told—
  Mapping my Past before those loving eyes,
With such minuteness that they might behold
  Each hair-line of my soul, without disguise?
Was Truth not woven, every line acrost—
  An iron thread through silver subtleties
Of Fancy or of Feeling, howe'er gloss'd?
  Was Faith not there, at rein or helm the while,
A guide, a check, for fancy's luring smile,
  A guide, a check, for feeling passion-toss'd?
Oh, how then, now, can thought of me so vile,
  Thought as of one to truth and faith both lost,
Ignobly come thy bosom to beguile,
  And kill affection with suspicion's frost!

XVI.

Nay, plead not thou art dull to-night,
  When I can see the tear-drop stealing,
Soft witness to love's watchful sight,
  Some lurking grief within revealing.
Wouldst thou so cheat the friend thou lovest
  Of half the wealth he owns in thee?
Why, sweet one, by that smile thou provest
  Thy tears as well belong to me!

Ah, tears again!—well, let them flow,
  In tenderness thus flow for ever,
Those last upon my breast I know
  Fresh from affection's fruitful river.
What! smiles once more!—Sweet April wonder,
  Thy sun and rain thou wilt not miss;
Why should not I then have my thunder,
  And melt each bolt into a kiss?

XVII.

Life seems to thee more earnest, dearest!
  And is it not the same with me?
Why, sweet, each shadow that thou fearest
  To me becomes reality—
A thought—a pang to mar my gladness,
And cloud my brow with tender sadness—
  And all of loving thee!

The jest from which thou often turnest
  Is only love's fond thoughtful guile,
And comes from heart in love most earnest
  When it would make thee smile—
Is but the stream's bright circles breaking
Beneath thy blessed tear-drops—waking
  Love's dimples there the while.

XVIII.

Thou ask'st me why that thought of death
  Should rise within our souls the same—
Why now, when dearer grows each breath
  Of life, we shrink not at his name!

What is it, sweet, but faith in each
  The other could not live alone?
What but the wish at once to reach
  The land where change is never known?

As, parted here, we dare not think
  Of wearying years to come between!
Nay, start not, love, as on the brink
  Of what may be—as it hath been—
We only part like twin-born rays
  Diverging from the morning sun,
Again within his orb to blaze
  When fused in heaven into one.

XIX.

Ask me not why I should love her,
  Look upon those soulful eyes!
Look while earth or feeling move her,
  And see there how sweetly rise
Thoughts gay and gentle from a breast
Which is of innocence the nest—
Which, though each joy were from it shred,
By truth would still be tenanted!

See from those sweet windows peeping,
  Emotions tender, bright, and pure,
And wonder not the faith I'm keeping
  Every trial can endure!
Wonder not that looks so winning
Still for me new ties are spinning;
Wonder not that heart so true
Keeps mine from ever changing too.

XX.

While he thou lovest were not the same,
If scathless all from passion's flame,
Wouldst thou the temper'd steel forego
At thought of what hath made it so?
Wouldst thou have bann'd the sun to shine
In spring upon thy chosen pine,
And dwarf'd the stature of the tree
That thus had never shelter'd thee!

Think'st thou the dream by fancy sent,
The fervor by wild passion lent—
Think'st thou the wandering tenderness
That yearns each loving heart to bless—
That either or that all can be
The love my soul still kept for thee?
Still faithful kept, till thou or death
Should come to claim her inmost breath!

XXI.

Thoughts—wild thoughts! oh why will ye wander,
Wander away from the task that's before ye?
Heart—weak heart! ah why art thou fonder,
Fonder of her than ever of glory?
What though the laurel for thee hath no glitter,
What though thy soul never yearn'd for a name;
When did Love garland a brow that was fitter
To wake in Love's bosom the wild wish of fame?

Doth she not watch o'er thine every endeavor?
Leans not her heart in warm faith on thine own?

If thou sit doubting and dreaming for ever,
Too late thou'lt discover that her dream has flown!
Ay! though each thought that is tender and glowing
Hath yet no errand, save only to her—
She may forget thee, while time is thus flowing;
Thou waste thy worship—fond idolater!

XXII.

In dreams—in dreams she answers to my yearning,
And fondly lays her downy cheek to mine;
In dreams each night that faithful form returning
Will on my breast with sweet content recline:
Awhile my heart keeps time to her soft breathing,
Heaving in motion to her bosom heaving.

I wake—and oh, there is an inward sinking,
A drear soul-faintness coming o'er me then,
That through the livelong day but makes my thinking
One fond, fond aching thus to dream again,—
Soul—soul, where art thou through the day employ'd,
Only to fill at night my bosom's void?

XXIII.

Why should I murmur lest she may forget me?
Why should I grieve to be by her forgot?
Better, then, wish that she had never met me,
Better, oh far, she should remember not!

Yet that sad wish—ah, would it not come o'er her
Knew she the heart on which she now relies?
Strong it is only in beating to adore her—
Faint in the moment her lov'd image flies!

Why should I murmur lest she may forget me?
Would I not rather be remember'd not
Ere have her grieve that she had ever met me?
I only suffer if I am forgot!

XXIV.

They say that thou art alter'd, Amy,
They say that thou no more
Dost keep within thy bosom, Amy,
The faith that once it wore;

They tell me that another now
Doth thy young heart assail;
They tell me, Amy, too, that thou
Dost smile on his love tale.

But I—I heed them not, my Amy,
Thy heart is like my own;
And still enshrined in mine, my Amy,
Thine image lives alone:

Whate'er a rival's hopes have fed,
Thy soul cannot be moved
Till he shall plead as I have plead,
And love as I have loved.

XXV.

Take back then thy pledges,—and peace to that heart
In which faith like a shadow can come and depart!
From which love, that seems cherished most fondly to-day,
Is cast, without grieving, to-morrow away.

Such a heart it may sadden mine own to resign,
But it never was mated to mingle with mine.
Love another! Nay, shrink not—more wisely thou
wilt
If truth to thy plighted in thine eyes be guilt.

I claim not, I ask not one thought in thy breast
While that thought brings misgiving and doubt to the
rest.
If the heart that thus fails thee can bid me depart,
Take back all love's pledges,—and peace to that
heart!

XXVI.

They tell me that my trusting heart
Thy fondness is deceived in;
They say that thou all faithless art
Whom I so well believed in!
I heed not, reck not, what they say
So earnestly about thee;
I'd rather trust my soul away
Than for one moment doubt thee.

Like mine thy youth was early lost;
Thy vows too rashly plighted;
Thy budding life by wintry frost
Of grief untimely, blighted.
Devotion is most deep and pure
In souls by sorrow shaded,
And love like ours will still endure
When brighter ties have faded.

XXVII.

Alas! if she be false to me
It is for her alone I weep!
'Tis that in coming years I see
Her suffering from such frailty
Than *mine*, oh, far more deep!

So tender, yet so false withal,
So proud, and yet so frail,
Responding to each flatterer's call,
Loving, yet often blind to all
Of love that could not fail—
Oh who will watch her wayward soul,
Who minister when I am gone,
Who point her spirit to its goal,
Who with unwearying love console
That truth-abandon'd one?

XXVIII.

I knew not how I loved thee—no!
I knew it not till all was o'er—
Until thy lips had told me so—
Had told me I must love no more!
I knew not how I loved thee!—yet
I long had loved thee wildly well!
I thought 'twere easy to forget—
I thought a word would break the spell:

And even when that word was spoken,
Ay! even till the very last,
I thought, that spell of faith once broken,
I could not long lament the past.

Oh, foolish heart! Oh, feeble brain,
That love could thus deceive—subdue!
Since hope cannot revive again,
Why cannot memory perish too?

XXIX.

The conflict is over, the struggle is past,
I have look'd—I have loved—I have worship'd my last;
And now back to the world, and let fate do her worst
On the heart that for thee such devotion hath nurs'd—
To thee its best feelings were trusted away,
And life hath hereafter not one to betray.

Yet not in resentment thy love I resign;
I blame not—upbraid not one motive of thine;
I ask not what change has come over thy heart,
I reck not what chances have doom'd us to part;
I but know thou hast told me to love thee no more,
And I still must obey where I once did adore.

Farewell, then, thou loved one—oh! loved but too well,
Too deeply, too blindly, for language to tell—
Farewell! thou hast trampled love's faith in the dust,
Thou hast torn from my bosom its hope and its trust!
But if thy life's current with bliss it would swell,
I would pour out my own in this last fond farewell!

XXX.

We parted in kindness, but spoke not of parting;
We talk'd not of hopes that we both must resign;

I saw not her eyes, and but one teardrop starting
  Fell down on her hand as it trembled in mine:

Each felt that the past we could never recover,
  Each felt that the future no hope could restore,
She shudder'd at wringing the heart of her lover,
  I dared not to say I must meet her no more.

Long years have gone by, and the springtime smiles ever
  As o'er our young loves it first smiled in their birth;
Long years have gone by, yet that parting, oh! never
  Can it be forgotten by either on earth.

The note of each wild bird that carols toward heaven
  Must tell her of swift-winged hopes that were mine,
While the dew that steals over each blossom at even
  Tells me of the teardrop that wept their decline.

LOVE AND FAITH.

'TWAS on one morn in springtime weather,
  A rosy, warm, inviting hour,
That Love and Faith went out together,
  And took the path to Beauty's bower.
Love laugh'd and frolick'd all the way,
  While sober Faith, as on they rambled,

Allow'd the thoughtless boy to play,
But watch'd him, wheresoe'er he gambolled.

So warm a welcome, Beauty smiled
Upon the guests whom chance had sent her,
That Love and Faith were both beguiled
The grotto of the nymph to enter ;
And when the curtains of the skies
The drowsy hand of Night was closing,
Love nestled him in Beauty's eyes,
While Faith was on her heart reposing.

Love thought he never saw a pair
So softly radiant in their beaming ;
Faith deem'd that he could meet nowhere
So sweet and safe a place to dream in ;
And there, for life in bright content,
Enchain'd, they must have still been lying,
For Love his wings to Faith had lent,
And Faith he never dream'd of flying.

But Beauty, though she liked the child,
With all his winning ways about him,
Upon his Mentor never smiled,
And thought that Love might do without him ;
Poor Faith, abused, soon sighing fled,
And now one knows not where to find him ;
While mourning Love quick followed
Upon the wings he left behind him.

'Tis said that in his wandering
Love still around that spot will hover,

Like bird that on bewilder'd wing
  Her parted mate pines to discover;
And true it is that Beauty's door
  Is often by the idler haunted:
But, since Faith fled, Love owns no more
  The spell that held his wings enchanted.

THE BLIGHTED HEART.

WHEN the flowers of Friendship or Love have de-
  cay'd
In the heart that has trusted and once been betray'd,
No sunshine of kindness their bloom can restore,
For the verdure of feeling will quicken no more!

Hope, cheated too often when life's in its spring,
From the bosom that nursed it for ever takes wing,
And memory comes, as its promises fade,
To brood o'er the havoc that passion has made,—

As 'tis said that the swallow the tenement leaves
Where ruin endangers her nest in the eaves,
While the desolate owl takes her place on the wall,
And builds in the mansion that nods to its fall.

"L'Amour Sans Ailes."

YOUNG Love, when tender mood beset him,
  One morn to Lilla's casement flew,
Who raised it just so far to let him
  Blow half his fragrant kisses through.

Love brought no perch on which to rest,
  And Lilla had not one to give him,
And now the thought her soul distress'd
  What should she do?—Where would she leave him?

Love maddens to be thus half caught,
  His struggle Lilla's pain increases;
"He'll fly—he'll fly away (she thought),
  Or beat himself and wings to pieces."

"His wings! why them I do not want—
  The restless things make all this pother:"
Love tries to fly, but finds he can't,
  And nestles near her like a brother.

Plumeless, we call him *Friendship* now;
  Love smiles at acting such a part—
But what cares he for lover's vow
  While thus *perdu* near Lilla's heart?

Trust not Love.

Oh, trust not Love—the wayward boy,
But haste, if you'd detain him,
Ere time can beauty's bond destroy,
Or other eyes and lips decoy,
With Hymen to enchain him.

The humming-bird the blossom leaves
Whene'er its sweets are failing;
The silken web the spider weaves
Yields up the prey to which she cleaves,
When autumn winds are wailing.

And Love, when beauty's bloom decays,
Will spread his fickle pinion,
And prove the web in which he plays
Too weak against the rude world's ways
To hold the roving minion.

Then trust not Love—the wayward boy,
But haste, if you'd detain him,
Ere time can beauty's bond destroy,
Or other eyes and lips decoy,
With Hymen to enchain him.

THE REMONSTRANCE.

YOU give up the world! why, as well might the sun,
When tired of drinking the dew from the flowers,
While his rays, like young hopes, stealing off one by one,
Die away with the muezzin's last note from the towers,
Declare that he never would gladden again,
With one rosy smile, the young morn in its birth;
But leave weeping Day, with her sorrowful train
Of hours, to grope o'er a pall-cover'd earth.

The light of that soul, once so brilliant and steady,
So far can the incense of flattery smother
That, at thought of the world of hearts conquered already,
Like Macedon's madman, you weep for another!
Oh! if, sated with this, you would seek worlds untried,
And fresh as was ours, when first we began it,
Let me know but the sphere where you next will abide,
And that instant, for one, I am off for that planet.

Wake, Lady, Wake!

WRITTEN FOR AN AIR IN DER FREISCHUTZ.

WAKE, Lady, wake! the stars on high
Are twinkling in the vaulted sky,
The dew drops on the leafy spray
Are trembling in the moon's cold ray;
But what to me are dewy skies
And moon and stars, unless thine eyes
Will waken, to rival the heaven's blue,
And the stars and moon in their brightness too?

Wake, Lady, wake! the murmuring breeze
Is soft among the swaying trees;
And with the sound of brooks is heard
The note of evening's lonely bird:
But thy loved voice is sweeter far
Than whispering woods or breezes are,
Or the silver sound of the tinkling rill,
Or the plaintive call of the whippoorwill.

Wake, Lady! or my heart alone
Will, like a lute that's lost its tone,
To nature's touch refuse to sound,
While all her works rejoice around
How can I prize the brightest spot,
If I am there, but thou art not?
Then while through thy lattice the moonbeams break,
'Tis thy lover that calls thee, wake, Lady, wake!

SERENADE.

SLEEPING! why now sleeping?
The moon herself looks gay,
While through thy lattice peeping;
Wilt not her call obey?
Wake, love, each star is keeping
For thee its brightest ray;
And languishes the gleaming
From fire-flies now streaming
Athwart the dewy spray.

Awake, the skies are weeping
Because thou art away,
But if of me thou'rt dreaming,
Sleep, loved one, while you may!
And music's wings shall hover
Softly thy sweet dreams over,
Fanning dark thoughts away,
While, dearest, 'tis thy lover
Who'll bid each bright one stay.

THE COQUETTE.

WE parted at the midnight hour,
We parted *then* as lovers part,
The stars which pierced that trellis'd bower,
They saw me press her to my heart;
I left her with no fear,—no doubt!
I left her with my hopes—my all—

I left her then! O God!—without
  A dream of what would soon befall.

I went to toil—far from her sight,
  Far from her blessed voice away—
But still she haunted me by night,
  Still murmur'd in my ears by day.
The hours flew by in dreams of her,
  Those hours which claim'd far other care,
I wasted them—fond worshipper—
  In dreams, whose waking was despair!

A month—no, not a month—by Heaven!
  Had fled since she was pledged to me—
Since *I* love's parting kiss had given
  To seal *her* vows of constancy!
The very moon was not yet old,
  Whose crescent beam our loves had lighted—
Yet ere those few short weeks were told,
  She had forgot the faith she plighted!

I heard her lips that faith forswear—
  And, while those lips revealed the tale,
My very soul it blush'd that e'er
  It could have loved a thing so frail!
Yet scorn—it was not scorn that stung—
  'Twas pity—horror—grief, that moved me—
I felt the wrong—the shameless wrong,
  But spared the heart that once had loved me!

Yes, faithless, false, as now I found it,
  That heart had beat against my own,

And I—I could not bear to wound it,
  When all its shielding worth was flown.
What though I could believe no more
  In *such* as her own lips reveal'd her!
Yet still when all Love's faith was o'er,
  Love's tenderness remained to shield her.

And when the moment came to break
  The subtle chain around me cast,
Like me she seem'd in soul to ache
  At riving of its links at last.
Could they betray my mind once more,
  Those pleading looks? yes! even then,
So sweet the guise of truth they wore,
  I *wish'd* to be deceived again.

Ay! strangely as at first we met—
  There did, by Heaven! around her hover
Such light of warmth and truth, that yet
  I, at the last, was still her lover!
And when I saw her brow o'ercast—
  Saw tears from those soft eyelids melt,
I reck'd not, cared not for the past,
  But there, adoring, could have knelt!

That moment to her lip and eye
  There came that calm and loveless air,
Like Beauty, when her triumph's nigh,
  Will toward its easy victim wear.
No test—no time—no fate had wrought
  O'er soul like mine so strong a spell,
As in that moment chill'd to naught
  Love that did seem unquenchable!

We parted—not as lovers part—
  No kind farewell—no fond regret
Was utter'd *then* from either heart—
  We parted only to forget;
We parted, not as lovers part,
  As lovers we can meet no more.
Let Time decide in either heart
  Which most such parting shall deplore.

THE WISH.

BRIGHT as the dew, on early buds that glistens,
  Sparkles each hope upon thy flower-strewn
    path;
Gay as a bird to its new mate that listens,
  Be to thy soul each winged joy it hath;
Thy lot still lead through ever-blooming bowers,
And Time for ever talk to thee in flowers.

Adored in youth, while yet the summer roses
  Of glowing girlhood bloom upon thy cheek,
And, loved not less when fading, there reposes
  The lily, that of springtime past doth speak.
Ne'er from Life's garden to be rudely riven,
But softly stolen away from Earth to Heaven.

WALLER TO SACHARISSA.

It is said they met at court after Waller was wedded to another, and that the lady coolly asked the poet to address a copy of verses to her: Johnson has commented upon the bitterness of his reply.

TO-NIGHT! to-night! what memories to-night
  Came thronging o'er me as I stood near thee.
Thy form of loveliness, thy brow of light,
    Thy voice's thrilling flow,
All, all were there; to me—to me as bright
  As when they claim'd my soul's idolatry
    Years, long years ago!

That gulf of years! O God! hadst thou been mine,
  Would all that's precious have been swallow'd there?
Youth's meteor hope, and manhood's high design,
    Lost, lost, for ever lost—
Lost with the love that with them all would twine,
  The love that left no harvest but despair.
    Unwon at such a cost!

Was it *ideal* that wild, wild love I bore thee?
  Or thou thyself—didst *thou* my soul enthral?
Such as thou art to-night did I adore thee!
    Ay, idolize—in vain!
Such as thou art to-night—could time restore me
  That wealth of loving—shouldst *thou* have it all
    To waste perchance again?

No! Thou didst break the coffers of my heart,
  And set so lightly by the hoard within,
That I too learn'd at last the squanderer's art,—
    Went idly here and there,
Filing my soul and lavishing a part
  On each, less cold than thou, who cared to win
    And seemed to prize a share.

No! Thou didst wither up my flowering youth.
  If blameless, still the bearer of a blight!
The unconscious agent of the deadliest ruth
    That human heart hath riven!
Teaching the scorn of my own spirit's truth!
  Holding—not *me*—but that fond worship light
    Which link'd my soul to heaven!

No!—No!—For me the weakest heart before
  One so untouch'd by tenderness as thine!
Angels have enter'd through the frail tent door
    That pass the palace now—
And HE who spake the words, "Go sin no more,"
  'Mid human passions saw the spark divine,
    But not in such as THOU!

THE SUICIDE.

A FRAGMENT.

"Put out the light, and then," &c.—SHAKSPEARE.

HE roam'd, an Arab on life's desert waste—
Its waters fleeting when they seemed most near—
Love's phantom leaving, when long vainly chased—
No aim to animate, no hope to cheer.

His was a heart where love, when once it sprung,
With every feeling would its tendrils twine;
And still it grew, though baffled, crush'd and wrung,
Rankly, as round an oak some noxious vine,

Within the poisonous folds of whose embrace
Withers each generous shoot that quickens there,
Till the proud features we no more can trace,
Which once that noble stem was wont to wear.

And time pass'd on—Time who both joy and grief
Bears on his tireless wings alike away,
As storms the bursting bud and wither'd leaf
Will sweep together from the fragile spray.

Her form matured, with all its girlish grace,
A woman's softer full proportion wore;
And none could look upon that radiant face,
And not the soul enthroned there adore.

Her eye was bright, or should a thought of him
Its laughing lustre for a moment shade,

'Twas but a passing cloud which could not dim
  The buoyant spirit in its beams that play'd.

And others bow'd where he before had knelt,
  And she to one, who even at such a shrine
Could only feign what he alone had felt,
  Did the rich guerdon of her heart resign.

She loved him for—for God knows what—'tis true
  In Fashion's field a brilliant name he'd earn'd;
And, with his full-dress pantaloons on too,
  His legs and compliments were both well turn'd.

We love, we know not why—in joy or sadness
  We waste on one the fountains of the heart,
The mind's best energies, the—pshaw!—'tis madness—
  'Tis worse than frenzy—'tis an idiot's part.

This Bertram knew—for his was not the dreaming
  Cherish'd illusion of a feeble mind;
He knew, too, that in hours there's no redeeming
  A soul like his from bonds which years have twined.

That she ne'er loved him, came the cold assurance
  Home to his heart, when all its springs were wasted;
He felt that his had been the vain endurance
  Of pangs to her unknown—by her untasted.

Dazzled by the prize his soul, his senses ravish'd,
  Rashly he ventured on a dangerous game ;
Lost, beyond hope, the stake so madly lavish'd,
  And felt his folly was alone to blame.

And then he knew they had not each been weighing
  An equal hazard in the chance gone by:
She had but been with the heart's counters playing—
  He, he had set his all upon a die.

But to what purpose now avail'd the seeing
  That love, such as ne'er did human pulses stir—
Which was to him the very food of being—
  Was but as pastime and a toy to her?

Her empire o'er his soul had been too deeply founded,
  Too long establish'd to reconquer now;
Still was she doom'd to be the heaven which bounded
  The world of all his hopes and fears below.

And were it not so, could the charm around him
  Even by a word of his at last be broken,
Fully as now that spell would yet have bound him—
  That magic word would still remain unspoken.

One night it chanced, when homeward sadly stray-
    ing,
  Beneath her window that he paused, unmoved,
To watch the light which, through the casement
    playing,
  At times was darken'd by the form he loved—

When through the half-raised sash, the summer air
  Brought, through the blind which screened the
    lady's bower,
Words to the throbbing ear, which listen'd there,
  That told him first it was her bridal hour!

The sounds of revelry had ceased—the lights
  Were all extinguish'd, except one alone;
'Tis that, 'tis that his straining vision blights,
  Dimly as through the half-shut blind it shone!

That little light! The burning Afric sun,
  Which pour'd its fierce and scorching noonday
    blaze
The heroic Roman's lidless eyes upon,
  Was not more maddening than that taper's rays.

The light's removed—but still a shadow dim
  Upon the curtain's folds reflected falls!
The light's extinguished—and the world to him
* * * * * * * *

LOVE'S VAGARIES.

I.

'TWAS wrongly done, to let her know the feeling
  Which mask'd so long within my heart lay hid,
Yet now I wonder at so well concealing
  My soul's full tenderness, as long I did;—
'Twas wrongly done—and yet, howe'er it move
  Her fervid nature thus to love in vain,
'Twere better vainly even thus to love
  Than not to know she was beloved again!

Those hours of passion now for ever pass'd,
  Those wild endearments that we oft have known,
Needed they not the veil around them cast
  That love, acknowledged love, at last hath thrown?
Long in remembrance as they now may live,
  However sad that living place may be,
That love a hallow'd tenderness will give
  To things all bitter else in memory.

II.

In dreams—in dreams she answers to my yearning,
  And fondly lays her downy cheek to mine;
In dreams each night that faithful form returning
  Will on my breast with sweet content recline:
Awhile my heart keeps time to her soft breathing,
Heaving in motion to her bosom heaving.

I wake—and oh, there is an inward sinking,
  A drear soul-faintness coming o'er me then,
That through the livelong day but makes my thinking
  One fond, fond aching thus to dream again,—
Soul—soul, where art thou through the day employ'd,
  Only to fill at night my bosom's void?

III.

What though I sigh to think that after all
  'Twas half some erring fancy of the mind,
Half that illusion which they "love" miscall
  Whose sense dreams not of sentiment refined?—
They to whom ne'er that gush of soul was given
Which melts the heart to mould it but for Heaven—

What though to think it was but this perchance
  Prompts the half-wistful—half-disdainful sigh;
Makes the fond tone—the tear—the tender glance
  Seem less than valueless in memory:
Still would I rather my love run to waste
Than she I love "love's bitterness" should taste.

THINK OF ME, DEAREST.

THINK of me, dearest, when day is breaking
  Away from the sable chains of night,
When the sun, his ocean-couch forsaking,
Like a giant first in strength awaking,
  Is flinging abroad his limbs of light;
As the breeze that first travels with morning forth,
Giving life to her steps o'er the quickening earth—
As the dream that has cheated thy soul through the
    night,
Let me come fresh in thy thoughts with the light.

Think of me, dearest, when day is sinking
  In the soft embrace of twilight gray,
When the starry eyes of heaven are winking,
And the weary flowers their tears are drinking,
  As they start like gems on the star-lit spray.
Let me come warm in thy thoughts at eve,
As the glowing track which the sunbeams leave,
When they, blushing, tremble along the deep
While stealing away to their place of sleep.

Think of me, dearest, when round thee smiling
  Are eyes that melt while they gaze on thee;
When words are winning and looks are wiling,
And those words and looks, of *others*, beguiling
  Thy fluttering heart from love and me.
Let me come, true in thy thoughts in that hour;
Let my trust and my faith—my devotion—have
    power,
When all that can lure to thy young soul is nearest,
To summon each truant thought back to me, dearest.

PLATONICS.

A PLACE for me—one place for me,
  Within the young wild heart be kept;
Howe'er Affection's chords may there
  By other hands than mine be swept;
However unto Love's mad thrill
  Their music may responsive be,
As now let sober Friendship still
  Preserve one note—one place for me.

When thy bright spirit grave, or gay,
  Some other chains delighted near,
To catch thy features' varying play,
  And watch each lightning thought appear,
However thou his soul mayst touch,
  Let him not wholly thine enthral
From one who ever loved so much
  To chase its meteor windings all.

When 'mid some scene where Nature flings
  Her loveliest enchantments round,
And in thy kindling soul upsprings
  Thoughts which no mortal breast can bound,
Or when upon some deathless page
  Thy mind communes with kindred mind,
Still let me there one thought engage,
  And round thy soaring spirit wind.

When first the bride-like dawn is blushing
  Within the arms of joyous Day,
Or when the twilight dews are hushing
  His footsteps o'er the hills away,
When from the fretted vault above
  God's ever burning lamps are hung,
And when in dreams of Heaven and love
  His mercies are around thee flung.

A place for me—one place for me,
  Within thy memory live enshrined,
Whatever idols Time may raise
  Upon the altars of thy mind.
And while youth's hopes before me sweep,
  Like bubbles on a freshening sea,
My bark of life shall ever keep
  One sacred berth for thee—for thee.

"COMING OUT"—A DREAM.

YOUNG Lesbia slept. Her glowing cheek
Was on her polish'd arm reposing,
And slumber closed those fatal eyes
Which keep so many eyes from closing.

For even Cupid, when fatigued
Of playing with his bow and arrows,
Will harmless furl his weary wings,
And nestle with his mother's sparrows.

Young Lesbia slept—and visions gay
Before her dreaming soul were glancing
Like sights that in the moonbeams show,
When fairies on the green are dancing.

And, first, amid a joyous throng
She seem'd to move in festive measure,
With many a courtly worshipper,
That waited on her queenly pleasure.

And then, by one of those strange turns
That witch the mind so when we're dreaming,
She was a planet in the sky,
And they were stars around her beaming.

Yet hardly had that lovely light
(To which one cannot here help kneeling)
Its radiance in the vault above
Been for a few short hours revealing,

When, like a blossom from the bough,
  By some remorseless whirlwind riven,
Swiftly upon its lurid path
  'Twas back to earth like lightning driven.

Yet, brightly still, though coldly, there
  Those other stars were calmly shining,
As if they did not miss the rays
  That were but now with theirs entwining.

And half with pique, and half with pain,
  To be from that gay chorus parting,
Young Lesbia from her dream awoke
  With swelling heart and teardrop starting.

INTERPRETATION.

Had she but thought of those below,
  Who thus were left with breasts benighted,
Till Heaven dismiss'd that star to earth,
  By which alone our hearts are lighted—

Or, had she recollected, when
  Each virtue from the world departed,
How Hope, the dearest, came again,
  And stay'd to cheer the lonely-hearted:

Sweet Lesbia could not thus have grieved
  From that cold, dazzling throng to sever,
And yield her young warm heart again
  To those that prize its worth for ever.

THE LOVER'S STAR.

DANISH AIR.

OH, when, 'mid thy wild fancy's dreaming,
Life's meteors around thee are streaming,
Thy tears still belie the false beaming
That fain would thy spirit control—
Look, look to that lone light above thee,
The star that seems set there to love thee,
Look there, and I am with thee in soul!
Look, look, etc.

And if, when thus wilder'd, thou turnest
To lean on the true and the earnest—
The friend for whom vainly thou yearnest
Has pass'd like a mist from life's strand.
Oh, come, come again to me, dearest!
Thou still to my soul shalt be nearest,
All mine in that bright spirit-land!
Oh! come, come again, etc.

TO A LADY.

WITH A COLLECTION OF VERSES.

A PASSING sigh, perhaps—perchance a sneer—
Is all these lines, if ever read, may claim;
And the wild thoughts, so vainly written here,
A worldly mind, perhaps, will calmly name
The sickly record of "a stripling's flame."

Yet, Lady, should you chance when years are fled,
Some hour when Memory from each burial-place
Gives up once more her long-forgotten dead,
Recalls the looks of each familiar face,
And in the heart renews each time-worn trace—

At such an hour, when others claim the sigh
Remembrance gives to early ties decay'd,
To hopes and fears now gone for ever by,
To scenes in memory's twilight charms array'd,
And loves and friendships long ago betray'd—

Should you then chance these faded lines to meet,
I know they will thy transient gaze arrest;
And he whose heart while yet Hope's pulses beat
Was thine, within thy pensive breast
Will claim one gentle thought among the rest.

Writing for an Album.

I'LL try no more—'tis all in vain
To rack for wit my head,
Wit left the mansion of my brain
When ye inhabited.
Thoughts will not come—words will not flow
Except when thus toward thee they go.

Oh! thou wert born to be my blight,
My bane upon this earth—
Fate did my doom that moment write
In which those eyes had birth.

'Tis strange that aught so good, so pure,
Should work the evil I endure.

Thou darkenest each hope that flings
O'er life one sunny ray;
And to each joy thou lendest wings
To take itself away.
Yet hope and joy—oh what to me
Are they, unless they spring from thee!

I'll try no more—'tis all in vain
To rack for wit my head,
While every chamber of my brain
By thee is tenanted.
Thoughts will not come—words will not flow
Except when thus toward thee they go.

To a Lady Weeping in Church.

WHEN tears from such as thee bedew the cheek,
In scenes like this—'twould seem that heavenly eyes
The soften'd glories of religion speak,
And claim the dewdrop from their kindred skies.

'Tis said that female saints of other days
From grovelling guilt could purge the foulest breast,
And teach the poor deluded wretch the ways
That lead to mansions of eternal rest.

And who could look upon thy heavenly face,
  Nor feel his breast with sacred fervor glow;
While every tear that fell from thee would chase
  Each thought that link'd him to this world below.

If then one tear of thine—one murmur'd sigh,
  Can tune the heart to sacred scenes like this,
Why doubt the power to lure the soul on high,
  And lead it captive to the realms of bliss?

Holding a Girl's Jumping Rope.

'TIS true thou art no silken band
  That knits my own with Zoe's hand,
    No fairy's chosen fetter;
Yet love himself, if *strength* alone
Were in his shackles to be shown,
    Could hardly find a better.

Thy stoutly twisted hempen strand
Would hang each felon in the land
    As high as e'er was Haman;
And—unless heavier than his head
Are hearts by love inhabited,
    Would hold the wildest Damon.

But thou—like rods magicians bear,
Of secret power art not aware,
    Nor yet to trace art able
The story of one coil that lingers
So lovingly on Zoe's fingers—
    Thou highly favor'd cable!

Since first in June, when hemp is green,
And bees and butterflies are seen
  Along its blossoms sailing,
Through mellow Autumn's jocund hours,
When warblers from the brown wood's bowers
  Are on its seeds regaling—

Till steadying on some top-mast spar
The footsteps of the gallant tar,
  Upon the wave careering,
Or pendent from the stately mast,
Through glowing palms thy cordage pass'd,
  Some banner bold uprearing.

'Tis strange that aught so void of life
Should have, as if with feeling rife,
  The electric power to mingle
The pulses that, upon my word,
I felt just now, together stirr'd,
  Through all thy twistings tingle.

The Declaration.

I LEFT the hall, as late it wore,
And glad to be in her boudoir
  From surveillance exempt, I
Gazed on the books she last had read,
The chair her form had hallowed,
  And grieved that it was empty.

And sleep his web was round me weaving
While listening to that wind-harp's breathing,
  Whose melody so wild is,
When one, whose charms are not of earth
(Her father just a *plum* is worth,
  And she his only child is),

With stealthy step before me stood,
As if to kiss in mad-cap mood
  My eyes, in slumber folded.
Her form was full—too full, you'd say,
And marvel at the graceful play
  Of charms so plumply moulded.

Her eyes were of a liquid blue,
Like sapphires limpid water through
  Their soften'd lustre darting;
Her mind-illumined brow was white
As snow-drift in the pale moonlight;
  The hair across it parting

Was of that paly brown, we're told
By poets takes a tinge of gold
  When sunbeams through it tremble,
While round her mouth two dimples play'd
Like—nothing e'er on earth was made
  Those dimples to resemble.

And there she stood in girlish glee
To win a pair of gloves, or see
  How odd I'd look when waking,

When I her round and taper waist
So unexpectedly embraced,
   The bond there was no breaking.

Her snowy bosom swell'd as though
The lava there beneath the snow
   Would heave it from its moorings;
Her eye seem'd half with anger fired,
And half with tenderness inspired
   In lightning-like endurings.

But when I loosed the eager grasp
In which I to my breast did clasp
   Her struggling and unwilling,
I felt somehow her fragile fingers
(The tingling in my own yet lingers)
   Within my pressure thrilling.

I spoke to her—she answer'd not—
I told her—now I scarce know what—
   I only do remember
My feelings when in words express'd,
Though warm as August in my breast,
   Seem'd colder than December.

But how can words the thoughts express
Of love so deep, so measureless
   As that which I have cherish'd!
O God! if my sear'd heart had given
The same devotedness to Heaven,
   It would not thus have perish'd!

I said, "You know—you must have known—
I long have loved—loved you alone,
  But cannot know how dearly."
I told her if my hopes were cross'd,
My every aim in life was lost—
  She knew I spoke sincerely!

She answer'd—as I breathless dwelt
Upon her words, and would have knelt—
  "Nay, move not thus the least;
You have—you long have had"—"Say on,
Sweet girl! thy heart?"—"Your foot upon
  The flounce of my *battiste.*"

CLOSING ACCOUNTS.

I PLACED—it was not ten years since—
  Sweet coz, a heart within thy keeping,
In which there was no pulse of prince,
  Of poet, or of hero, leaping,
But it was generous, warm and true,
  True to itself, and true to thee:
And toward thine own it fondly drew—
  Drew almost in idolatry.

I came to thee when years had fled,
  To learn how well the charge was kept;
That heart—it was so altered,
  Upon the change I could have wept:

The buoyant hope, the daring aim,
  The independence, stern and high;
Spirit, misfortune could not tame,
  And pride that might the worst defy—

All, all were gone—and in their stead
  Were bitter and were blasted feelings:
And thoughts Despair so far had led
  They shudder'd at their own revealings.
Yet I—although Distrust did prey
  Within that heart so wildly then
It ate the better half away,
  I left the rest with thee again.

Perhaps that heart in worthier case,
  I thought thou wouldst at last restore;
Perhaps I hoped thou mightst replace
  With thine, the one abused before:
Perhaps there was—the truth as well
  May out at once—perhaps there was in
Those matchless eyes so strong a spell
  I could not help it, witching cousin.

Well, it was thine—thine only still,
  A little worse, perhaps, for wear;
But firm, despite of every ill
  Which Fate and thou had gather'd there.
Yet now, when Youth and Hope are past,
  And care will soon make manhood gray,
I think—I think from thee at last
  That I must take that heart away.

Still, if it grieve thee to restore
 A trust that's held so carelessly,
Or if, when asking back once more
 The heart I left in pledge with thee,
It may, in spite of all I've said,
 By some odd chance with thine be blended,
Why, cousin, give me that instead,
 And all our business here is ended.

The Loon upon the Lake.

FROM THE CHIPPEWAY.

I LOOK'D across the water,
 I bent over it and listen'd,
I thought it was my lover,
 My true lover's paddle glisten'd.
Joyous thus his light canoe would the silver ripples wake.
But no, it is the Loon alone—the Loon upon the lake,
Ah me! it is the Loon alone—the Loon upon the lake.

I see the fallen maple
 Where he stood, his red scarf waving,
Though waters nearly bury
 Boughs they then were newly laving.
I hear his last farewell, as it echoed from the brake.
But no, it is the Loon alone—the Loon upon the lake,
Ah me! it is the Loon alone—the Loon upon the lake.

TRANSLATION OF AN INDIAN LOVE SONG.

I.

FAIREST of flowers by fountain or lake,
Listen, my fawn-eyed one, wake, oh awake!
Pride of the prairies, one look from thy bower
Will gladden my spirits like dew-drops the flower.

II.

Thy glances to music my soul can attune,
As sweet as the murmur of young leaves in June;
Then breathe but a whisper from lips that disclose
A balm like the morning or autumn's last rose.

III.

My pulse leaps toward thee like fountains when first
Through their ice chains in April toward Heaven they burst;
Then, fairest of flowers, by forest or lake,
Listen, my fawn-eyed one, wake, oh awake!

IV.

Like this star-paved water where clouds o'er it lower,
If thou frownest, beloved, is my soul in that hour;
But when Heaven and thou, love, your smiles will unfold,
If the current be ruffled, its ripples are gold.

V.

Awake, love; all nature is smiling, yet I,
I cannot smile, dearest, when thou art not by;

Look from thy bower then, here on the lake,
Pulse of my beating heart, wake, oh awake!

To a Lady

WHO TALKED OF COMMUNING WITH THE STARS WHEN SHE WAS SAD.

OH tell not the stars, the gay stars, of thy sadness,
If moments there be when the feeling steals o'er thee;
They may shine like the world o'er thy moments of gladness,
And gild each bright thought with a ray of their glory,
But their beams are too cold and too far off for sorrow
To awaken a sigh from their chorus of mirth,
And the soul that in sadness would sympathy borrow
Must look for a lender much nearer the earth.
Then lavish no more on those chilly orbs yonder,
The treasures of feeling they cannot return;
Awhile on the planet from which thy thoughts wander,
There is one heart, at least, will with sympathy burn.

TASSO TO LEONORA.

STILL, still I love thee; Hope no more,
 'Tis true, may light my dungeon's gloom,
And youth as well as hope is o'er,
 Both buried in a living tomb;
And even reason doth forsake me,
 So oft that I begin to fear
If not the madman they would make me,
 Its utter loss is ever near;
Yet fettered in this hideous cell,
 And banned and barred from those sweet eyes,
Unknowing if one memory dwell
 With thee of him who daily dies,—
Still, Leonora, still alone to thee
Beneath their shackles still untamably
Love's pulses beat as if my limbs were free.

Go tell thy brother though the infectious breath
Of my rank prison may be steeped in death,
Though through my veins corrupting now may steal
The accursed taint which day by day I feel
Poisoning life's tabernacle, regret
For having loved thee, Leonora, never yet,
In spite of all I've borne or yet may bear,
Hath wrung one craven tear from my despair.
And thou—thou who from him who'd do and dare,
And suffer all of anguish heart can feel
Thou who in beauty's pride did shrink to hear
The love that lips could only half reveal;
Blushing, ashamed, because thou wert so dear

To one thy kinsman cared not to approve,—
Thou, Leonora, when I am no more,
Shalt feel the influence of a poet's love;
In every land my story they'll deplore,
Pilgrims from all shall make my grave their shrine,
And each who breathes my name shall murmur thine.

St. Valentine's Day.

THE snow yet in the hollow lies;
  But, where by shelvy hill 'tis seen,
In myriad rills it trickling flies
  To lace the slope with threads of green;
Down in the meadow glancing wings
  Flit in the sunshine round a tree,
Where still a frosted apple clings,
  Regale for early Chickadee:

And chestnut buds begin to swell,
  Where flying squirrels peep to know
If from the tree-top, yet, 'twere well
  To sail on leathery wing below—
As gently shy and timorsome,
  Still holds she back who should be mine;
Come, Spring, to her coy bosom, come,
  And warm it toward her Valentine!

Come, Spring, and with the breeze that calls
  The wind-flower by the hill-side rill,

The soft breeze that by orchard walls
  First dallies with the daffodil—
Come lift the tresses from her cheek,
  And let me see the blush divine,
That mantling there, those curls would seek
  To hide from her true Valentine.

Come, Spring, and with the Red-breast's note,
  That tells of bridal tenderness,
Where on the breeze he'll warbling float
  Afar his nesting mate to bless—
Come, whisper, 'tis not always Spring!
  When birds may mate on every spray—
That April boughs cease blossoming!
  With love it is not always May!

Come, touch her heart with thy soft tale,
  Of tears within the floweret's cup,
Of fairest things that soonest fail,
  Of hopes we vainly garner up—
And while, that gentle heart to melt,
  Like mingled wreath, such tale you twine,
Whisper what lasting bliss were felt
  In lot shared with her Valentine.

THE BLUSH.

I COULD not wish that in thy bosom aught
  Should e'er one moment's transient pain awaken,
Yet can't regret that thou—forgive the thought—
  As flowers when shaken

Will yield their sweetest fragrance to the wind,
Should, ruffled thus, betray thy heavenly mind.

The lilies faintly to the roses yield,
  As on thy thoughtful cheek they straggling vie
(Who would not strive upon so sweet a field
  To win the mastery?),
And thoughts are in thy speaking eyes reveal'd,
Pure as the fount the prophet's rod unseal'd.

THY NAME.

IT comes to me when healths go round,
  And o'er the wine their garlands wreathing,
The flowers of wit, with music wound,
  Are freshly from the goblet breathing!
From sparkling song and sally gay
It comes to steal my heart away,
And fill my soul, mid festive glee,
With sad, sweet, silent thoughts of thee.

It comes to me upon the mart,
  Where care in jostling crowds is rife;
Where Avarice goads the sordid heart,
  Or cold Ambition prompts the strife;
It comes to whisper if I'm there,
'Tis but with thee each prize to share,
For Fame were not success to me,
Nor riches wealth unshared with thee.

It comes to me when smiles are bright
  On gentle lips that murmur round me,
And kindling glances flash delight
  In eyes whose spell might once have bound me.
It comes—but comes to bring alone
Remembrance of some look or tone,
Dearer than aught I hear or see,
Because 'twas worn or breathed by thee.

It comes to me where cloister'd boughs
  Their shadows cast upon the sod ;
Awhile in Nature's fane my vows
  Are lifted from her shrine to God ;
It comes to tell that all of worth
I dream in heaven, or know on earth,
However bright or dear it be,
Is blended with my thought of thee.

The Call of Spring.

THOU wak'st again, O Earth !
  From winter's sleep !—
Bursting with voice of mirth
    From icy keep ;
And laughing at the Sun,
Who hath their freedom won,
    Thy waters leap !

Thou wak'st again, O Earth !
    Feebly again,

And who by fireside hearth
    Will now remain?
Come on the rosy hours—
Come on thy buds and flowers,
As when in Eden's bowers,
    Spring first did reign.
Birds on thy breezes chime
Blithe as in that matin time
    Their choiring begun:
Earth, *thou* hast many a prime—
    Man hath but one!

Thou wak'st anew, O Earth!
    Freshly anew!
As when at Spring's first birth
    First flow'rets grew.
Heart! that to earth dost cling,
While boughs are blossoming,
    Why wake not too?

Long thou in sloth hast lain,
Listing to Love's soft strain—
    Wilt thou sleep on?
Playing, thou sluggard heart,
In life no manly part,
    Though youth be gone.
Wake! 'tis Spring's quickening breath
    Now o'er thee blown;
Awake thee! ere thou in death
Pulselessly slumbereth,
Pluck thou from Glory's wreath
    One leaf alone!

Written in a Lady's Prayer Book.

THY thoughts are Heavenward! and thy heart, they say,
Which love, oh more than mortal, failed to move,
Now in its precious casket melts away,
And owns the impress of a Saviour's love!

Many, in days gone by, full many a prayer,
Pure, though impassion'd, has been breathed for thee
By one who once thy hallow'd name would dare
Prefer with his to the Divinity.

Requite them now—not with an earthly love—
But since with that his lot thou mayst not bless,
Ask—what he dare not pray for from above—
For him the mercy of Forgetfulness.

Myne Heartte.

I SOMMETYMES thinnke thye womannes artte
Hathe fromme mye bosomme whytch'd my heartte,
Yt dothe soe oftenne feele to mee
Lyke caskette where no jewelles be,
Or, oceanne shelle wilk breathes dystresse
I ween fromme verye emptynesse;
And thenne I wishe sic faythless heartte
Of mee hadde never been a parte.

And sommetymes doe I thynnke yts tyde
Is bye thye coldness petryfyd,
Or, thatte thyne eyne scorche uppe ye sayme
Fromme healthfulle boundynges through mye frayme,
Yt laggs soe in its course lyke staynes,
Wilk blushynge creepe through cowardes veynes;
And thenne I thynke that sic an heartte
Of manne hadde bettere notte be parte.

And sommetymes doe I thynke 'twere welle
Thys heartte shouldde breake beneathe thye spelle,
Since lonnge yt onlye thoughtes of payne
Hathe sentte untoe my weary brainne.
Soe manaye that ye sabel suite
Dothe crowde mye reasonne fromme her seatte,
And mayke me thynnke I'd rayther parte
Wythe lyfe in sic an faythelesse heartte.

THE LOVE TEST.

I THOUGHT she was wayward—inconstant in part,
But thought not the weakness e'er reached to her heart;
'Twas a lightness of mood which but tempted a lover
The more the true way to that heart to discover.

What changeful seem'd there, was the play of the
wave
Which veileth the depth of the firm ocean cave;
I cared not how fitful that light wave might flow,
I would dive for the pearl of affection below.

I won it, methought! and now welcome the strife,
The burthen, the toil, the worst struggles of life;
Come trouble—come sorrow—come pain and despair,
We divide ills, that each for the other would bear!

I *believed*—I could SWEAR—there was that in her
breast,
That soul of wild feeling, which needs but the test,
To leap like a falchion—bright, glowing, and true,
To the hand which its worth and its temper best
knew.

And what was the struggle which tested love's
power?
What fortune, so soon, could bring trial's dark hour?
Did some *shadow* of evil first make her heart quail?
Or the WORST prove at once that her truth could
ne'er fail?

I painted it sternly, the lot she might share!
I took from LOVE's wing all the gloss it may bear;
I told her how often his comrade is CARE!
I appeal'd to her *heart*—and her heart it was—
WHERE?

Seek not to Understand Her.

WHY seek her heart to understand,
  If but enough thou knowest
To prove that all thy love, like sand,
  Upon the wind thou throwest?
The ill thou makest out at last
Doth but reflect the bitter past,
While all the good thou learnest yet
But makes her harder to forget.

What matters all the nobleness
  Which in her breast resideth,
And what the warmth of tenderness
  Her mien of coldness hideth,
If but ungenerous thoughts prevail
When thou her bosom wouldst assail,
While tenderness and warmth doth ne'er
By any chance toward thee appear?

Sum up each token thou hast won
  Of kindred feeling there—
How few for Hope to build upon,
  How many for Despair!
And if e'er word or look declareth
Love or aversion which she beareth,
While of the first no proof thou hast,
How many are there of the last!

Then strive no more to understand
  Her heart, of which thou knowest

Enough to prove thy love, like sand,
  Upon the wind thou throwest:
The ill thou makest out at last
Doth but reflect the bitter past,
While all the good thou learnest yet
But makes her harder to forget.

WITHERING, WITHERING.

WITHERING—withering—all are withering—
  All of hope's flowers that youth hath nursed;
Flowers of love too early blossoming;
  Buds of ambition, too frail to burst.
Faintily—faintily—ah! how faintily
  I feel life's pulses ebb and flow:
Yet, sorrow, I know thou dealest daintily
  With one who should not wish to live moe.

Nay! why, young heart, thus timidly shrinking?
  Why doth thy upward wing thus tire?
Why are thy pinions so droopingly sinking,
  When they should only waft thee higher?
Upward—upward, let them be waving,
  Lifting thy soul toward her place of birth:
There are guerdons there more worth thy having,
  Far more thàn any these lures of earth.

"*Our Friendship.*"

IT *will* endure! It hath the seal upon it
  That once alone in life is ever set;
It will endure! we both by suffering won it!
  It will endure—for neither can forget.

It *must* endure! for is not Truth immortal?
  And those same tears which saw our hopes depart,
Brought her, the comforter, from Heaven's bright
    portal,
  In rainbow radiance spanning heart to heart!

---

*To a Waxen Rose.**

GO, mocking flower,
  Thou plastic child of art,
Back to thy lady's bower;
    Go and ask if thou,
    False one, art proven now
  An emblem of her heart?

Tell her, that like thee
  That heart's of little worth,
However kind it be,
    Which any hand with skill
    May mould unto its will:
  Too pliant from its birth.

* "Go, lovely rose."—Walle.

Go, cheating blossom,
  Scentless as morning dew,
Go ask if in her bosom,
  Although love's bud may be
  In brightness like to thee,
It owns no fragrance too.

But if fadeless, yet
  Still, still her love blooms on ;
Tell her—oh, ne'er forget
  To tell her, from my heart
  Affection will not part
When all life's flowers are gone.

Songs and Occasional Poems.

Songs and Occasional Poems.

Monterey.

"Pends toi Brave Crillon! Nous avons combattu, et tu n' y etois pas."—*Lettre de Henri IV. a Crillon.*

WE were not many—we who stood
  Before the iron sleet that day—
Yet many a gallant spirit would
Give half his years if he then could
  Have been with us at Monterey.

Now here, now there, the shot, it hailed
  In deadly drifts of fiery spray,
Yet not a single soldier quailed
When wounded comrades round them wailed
  Their dying shout at Monterey.

And on—still on our column kept
  Through walls of flame its withering way;
Where fell the dead, the living stept,
Still charging on the guns which swept
  The slippery streets of Monterey.

The foe himself recoiled aghast,
  When, striking where he strongest lay,

We swooped his flanking batteries past,
And braving full their murderous blast,
  Stormed home the towers of Monterey.

Our banners on those turrets wave,
  And there our evening bugles play;
Where orange boughs above their grave
Keep green the memory of the brave
  Who fought and fell at Monterey.

We are not many—we who press'd
  Beside the brave who fell that day;
But who of us has not confess'd
He'd rather share their warrior rest,
  Than not have been at Monterey?

The Men of Churubusco.

THEY'LL point them out in after years—
  The men of Churubusco fight!
And tender hearts will name with tears
  The gallant spirits quenched in night,
When each who under WINFIELD fought,
  And kept the field alive,
Was equal, in the deeds he wrought,
  To any common five—
They'll point them out, those veterans then,
As far beyond all common men,
And each to each, with stern delight,
Will name the Churubusco fight.

They'll sing their praise, when they're no more—
  The men of Churubusco fight!
And when their latest march is o'er—
  As one by one is lost to sight—
Then girls will beg his friends to spare,
  From off that hoary brow,
A shred but of the scattered hair
  Which waves so richly now:
And loiterers by the inn-side hearth
Will pause amid their tavern mirth,
And, filling, fear since he has pass'd,
They drink "to Churubusco's last!"

They'll paint their deeds in statued hall—
  The deeds of Churubusco's fight:
And on the smoke-dried cottage wall
  Will smile their pictures, brave and bright,
Who fought with stalwart Scott of yore,
  That storied field to win—
When every warrior bosom bore
  Five hero hearts within:
They'll legends tell of heroes then,
Far, far beyond all modern men,
And still in song will grow more bright
The deeds of Churubusco fight.

"*Rio Bravo.*"

A MEXICAN LAMENT.

Air.—Roncesvalles.

I.

RIO BRAVO! Rio Bravo! saw men ever such a sight
Since the field of Roncesvalles sealed the fate of many a knight.
Dark is Palo Alto's story—sad Resaca Palma's rout,
Ah me! upon those fields so gory how many a gallant life went out.
There our best and bravest lances shivered 'gainst the Northern steel,
Left the valiant hearts that couch'd them 'neath the Northern charger's heel.
Rio Bravo! Rio Bravo! brave hearts ne'er mourned such a sight,
Since the noblest lost their life-blood in the Roncesvalles fight.

II.

There Arista, best and bravest—there Raguena, tried and true,
On the fatal field thou lavest, nobly did all men could do;
Vainly there those heroes rally, Castile on Montezuma's shore,
Vainly there shone Aztec valor brightly as it shone of yore.

Rio Bravo! Rio Bravo! saw men ever such a sight,
Since the dews of Roncesvalles wept for Paladin
and knight.

III.

Heard ye not the wounded coursers shrieking on
yon trampled banks,
As the Northern wing'd artillery thundered on our
shattered ranks?
On they came—those Northern horsemen—on like
eagles toward the sun,
Followed then the Northern bayonet, and the field
was lost and won.
Rio Bravo! Rio Bravo! minstrel ne'er sung such a
fight,
Since the day of Roncesvalles sang the fame of
martyred knight.

IV.

Rio Bravo! fatal river! saw ye not, while red with
gore,
One cavalier all headless quiver, a nameless trunk
upon thy shore?
Other champions not less noted sleep beneath thy
sullen wave;
Sullen water, thou hast floated armies to an ocean
grave.
Rio Bravo! Rio Bravo! lady ne'er wept such a sight,
Since the moon of Roncesvalles kiss'd in death her
own loved knight.

V.

Weepest thou, lorn Lady Inez, for thy lover 'mid the slain?
Brave La Vega's trenchant sabre cleft his slayer to the brain—
Brave La Vega, who, all lonely, by a host of foes beset,
Yielded up his falchion only, when his equal there he met.
Oh, for Roland's horn to rally his Paladins by that sad shore!
Rio Bravo, Roncesvalles, ye are names linked evermore.

VI.

Sullen river! sullen river! vultures drink thy gory wave,
But they blur not those loved features, which not Love himself could save.
Rio Bravo, thou wilt name not that lone corse upon thy shore,
But in prayer sad Inez names him, names him praying evermore.
Rio Bravo! Rio Bravo! lady ne'er mourned such a knight,
Since the fondest hearts were broken by the Roncesvalles fight.

Le Faineant.

"NOW arouse thee, Sir Knight, from thine indolent ease,
Fling boldly thy banner abroad in the breeze,
Strike home for thy lady—strive hard for the prize,
And thy guerdon shall beam from her love-lighted eyes!"

"I shrink not the trial," that bluff knight replied—
"But I battle—not *I*—for an unwilling bride;
Where the boldest may venture to do and to dare,
My pennon shall flutter—my bugle peal there!

"I quail not at aught in the struggle of life,
I'm not all unproved even now in the strife;
But the wreath that I win, all unaided—alone,
Round a faltering brow it shall never be thrown!"

"Now fie on thy manhood, to deem it a sin
That she loveth the glory thy falchion might win!
Let them doubt of thy prowess and fortune no more;
Up! Sir Knight, for thy Lady—and do thy devoir!"

"She hath shrunk from my side, she hath failed in her trust,
Not relied on my blade, but remember'd its rust;
It shall brighten once more in the field of its fame,
But it is not for her I would now win a name."

The knight rode away, and the lady she sigh'd
When he featly as ever his steed would bestride,
While the mould from the banner he shook to the
wind
Seem'd to fall on the breast he left aching behind.

But the rust on his glaive and the rust in his heart
Had corroded too long and too deep to depart,
And the brand only brighten'd in honor once more,
When the heart ceased to beat on the fray-trampled
shore.

Rosalie Clare.

WHO owns not she's peerless—who calls her not
fair—
Who questions the beauty of Rosalie Clare?
Let him saddle his courser and spur to the field,
And though harness'd in proof, he must perish or
yield;
For no gallant can splinter—no charger may dare
The lance that is couch'd for young Rosalie Clare.

When goblets are flowing, and wit at the board
Sparkles high, while the blood of the red grape is
pour'd,
And fond wishes for fair ones around offer'd up
From each lip that is wet with the dew of the cup,—
What name on the brimmer floats oftener there,
Or is whisper'd more warmly, than Rosalie Clare?

They may talk of the land of the olive and vine—
Of the maids of the Ebro, the Arno, or Rhine;—
Of the Houris that gladden the East with their smiles,
Where the sea's studded over with green summer
isles;
But what flower of far-away clime can compare
With the blossom of ours—bright Rosalie Clare?

Who owns not she's peerless—who calls her not fair?
Let him meet but the glances of Rosalie Clare!
Let him list to her voice—let him gaze on her form—
And if, hearing and seeing, his soul do not warm,
Let him go breathe it out in some less happy air
Than that which is bless'd by sweet Rosalie Clare.

The Myrtle and Steel.

ἐν μύρτου τὸ κλαδὶ ξίφος φορήσω.—*Callistratus.*

ONE bumper yet, gallants, at parting,
One toast ere we arm for the fight;
Fill round, each to her he loves dearest—
'Tis the last he may pledge her, to-night!
Think of those who of old at the banquet
Did their weapons in garlands conceal,
The patriot heroes who hallow'd
The entwining of Myrtle and Steel!
Then hey for the Myrtle and Steel!
Then ho for the Myrtle and Steel!
Let every true blade that e'er loved a fair maid
Fill a round to the Myrtle and Steel.

'Tis in moments like this, when each bosom
With its highest-toned feeling is warm,
Like the music that's said from the ocean
To rise in the gathering storm,*
That her image around us should hover,
Whose name, though our lips ne'er reveal,
We may breathe through the foam of a bumper,
As we drink to the Myrtle and Steel.
Then hey for the Myrtle and Steel !
Then ho for the Myrtle and Steel !
Let every true blade that e'er loved a fair maid
Fill a round to the Myrtle and Steel.

Now mount, for our bugle is ringing
To marshal the host for the fray,
Where our flag to the firmament springing
Flames over the battle array :
Yet,—gallants—one moment—remember,
When your sabres the death-blow would deal,
That MERCY wears *her* shape who's cherished
By lads of the Myrtle and Steel.
Then hey for the Myrtle and Steel !
Then ho for the Myrtle and Steel !
Let every true blade that e'er loved a fair maid
Fill a round to the Myrtle and Steel.

* In Pascagoula Bay strange music is heard when certain winds prevail. Naturalists attribute the phenomenon to the vibration of the "horns" of catfish, which at such times congregate in large schools.

Algonquin War Song.

"PE NA SE-WUG."

HEAR not ye their shrill-piping
screams on the air?
Up! Braves, for the conflict
prepare ye—prepare!
Aroused from the canebrake,
far south, by your drum,
With beaks whet for carnage,
the Battle Birds come.

Oh, God of my fathers,
as swiftly as they,
I ask but to swoop
from the hills on my prey;
Give this frame to the winds,
on the Prairie below,
But my soul, like thy bolt,
I would hurl on the foe!

On the forehead of Earth
strikes the Sun in his might,
Oh gift me with glances
as searching as light,
In the front of the onslaught
to single each crest,
Till my hatchet grows red
on their bravest and best.

Why stand ye back idly,
ye Sons of the Lake!
Who boast of the scalp-locks
ye tremble to take?
Fear-dreamers may linger,
my skies are all bright—
On—on—to the War Path,*
MY GOD AND MY RIGHT.

Algonquin Death Song.

"A BE TUH GE ZHIG."

UNDER the hollow sky,
Stretch'd the Prairie lone,
Centre of glory, I
Bleeding, disdain to groan,
But like a battle cry
Peal forth thy thunder moan,
Baim-wa-wa! †

Star—Morning Star, whose ray
Still with the dawn I see,
Quenchless through half the day,
Gazing thou seest me;

* Hoh! Nemonedo netaibuatum o win.

† Baim-wa-wa means "the sound of passing thunders," a phrase which will convey a just idea of the violence of this figure, and the impossibility of rendering it into English by any single word.

Yon birds of carnage, they
Fright not my gaze from thee! *
Baim-wa-wa!

* The battle-fields of our Mexican war have given a new and terrible interest to this bold figure of the wounded Indian warrior. The following paragraph, which appeared in a New York journal a few days preceding the arrival of the news of the bloody field of Buena Vista, has all the interest of what the newspapers call "a curious coincidence."

Phenomenon in Natural History.—The Montgomery (Alabama) Journal says:

"An intelligent and reliable correspondent at Missouri, Pike county, informs us of a singular circumstance, which had somewhat troubled many of the worthy citizens of that section. This was the appearance of an immense flight of the great American vulture, of several miles in length, and containing millions of these aërial scavengers. They were a long time in passing, and at times darkened the whole horizon. The writer says they came nearly due north and steered nearly south; some flew so low as to be within the limits of the boughs of the tallest trees, and others so high as scarcely to be seen. At one time the whole canopy seemed to be darkened with these birds from east to west, north to south; from the tops of trees to as high as the sight could reach was one dark cloud.

"The question now is one of interest to naturalists, where such a vast number of these birds could have been bred, and why this passage, so unusual, from its known habits."

The Alabamian is evidently no poet, or he could not fail to have interpreted this "phenomenon" as the fearful augury of a great battle or raging pest in Mexico. Such a superstition as this is common among our Indian tribes, who call these birds "the battle birds."

"Aroused from the cane-brakes, far south, by your drum,
With beaks whet for carnage, the *Battle Birds* come,"

Bird, in thine airy rings
Over the foeman's line,
Why do thy flapping wings
Nearer me thus incline?
Blood of the dauntless brings *
Courage, O Bird, to thine!
Baim-wa-wa!

Hark to those Spirit-notes!
Ye high Heroes divine,
Hymned from your god-like throats
That song of Praise is mine!
Mine, whose grave pennon floats †
Over the foeman's line!
Baim-wa-wa!

are lines of an Indian war-song, of which the original is given in Schoolcraft's "Oneota."—*N. Y. Gazette.*

* *Nun-pah-shene*, or "The Dauntless," is a title given among some tribes of the Northwest to those fraternized bands of warriors, in which each member is consecrated to death on the battle-field, or rather is sworn never to desert a brother of the band in battle.

† The Indians plant flags at the head of the grave, which it is deemed sacrilegious even for an enemy to disturb.

These stanzas, says Mr. Schoolcraft, "have all been actually sung on warlike occasions, and repeated in my hearing. They have been gleaned from the traditionary songs of the Chippewas of the north, whose villages extend through the region of Lake Superior and the utmost sources of the Mississippi."

Sparkling and Bright.

SPARKLING and bright in liquid light
  Does the wine our goblets gleam in,
With hue as red as the rosy bed
  Which a bee would choose to dream in.
    Then fill to-night, with hearts as light,
      To loves as gay and fleeting
    As bubbles that swim on the beaker's brim,
      And break on the lips while meeting.

Oh! if Mirth might arrest the flight
  Of Time through Life's dominions,
We here awhile would now beguile
  The gray-beard of his pinions,
    To drink to-night, with hearts as light,
      To loves as gay and fleeting
    As bubbles that swim on the beaker's brim,
      And break on the lips while meeting.

But since delight can't tempt the wight,
  Nor fond regret delay him,
Nor Love himself can hold the elf,
  Nor sober Friendship stay him,
    We'll drink to-night, with hearts as light,
      To loves as gay and fleeting
    As bubbles that swim on the beaker's brim,
      And break on the lips while meeting.

BUFF AND BLUE.

Air—"Old Dan Tucker."

OH bold and true,
In buff and blue,
Is the soldier-lad that will fight for you.
In fort or field,
Untaught to yield,
Though death may close his story—
In charge or storm,
'Tis woman's form
That marshals him to glory.
For bold and true,
In buff and blue,
Is the soldier-lad that will fight for you.

In each fair fold
His eyes behold
When his country's flag waves o'er him—
In each rosy stripe,
Like her lip so ripe,
His girl is still before him.
For bold and true,
In buff and blue,
Is the soldier-lad that will fight for you.

"*Far Away.*"

Air—" Long time ago."

THE song—the song that once could move me
In life's glad day—
The song of her who used to love me
Far—far away—
It makes my sad heart, fonder—fonder—
Wildly obey
The spell that wins each thought to wander
Far—far away!

Once more upon my native river
The moonbeams play,
Once more the ripples shine as ever
Far—far away—
But ah, the friends who smiled around me,
Where—where are they!
Where the sweet spell, that early bound me,
Far—far away?

I think of all that hope once taught me—
Too bright to stay—
Of all that music fain had brought me,
Far—far away!
And weep to feel there's no returning
Of that glad day,
Ere all that brightened life's fresh morning
Was far—far away.

THE SLEIGH BELLS.

MERRILY, merrily sound the bells
  As o'er the ground we roll,
And the snow-drift breaks in silvery flakes
  Before our cariole.
When wrapp'd in buffalo soft and warm,
  With mantle and tippet dight,
We cheerily cleave the fleecy storm,
  Or skim in the cold moonlight.
Merrily, merrily! Merrily, merrily!
  Merrily sound the bells.

Merrily, merrily sound the bells
  Upon the wind without,
When the wine is mull'd and the waffle cull'd,
  And the song is passed about.
While rosy lips and dimpled cheeks
  The welcome joke inspire,
And mirth in many a bright eye speaks
  Around the hickory fire.
Merrily, merrily! Merrily, merrily!
  Merrily sound the bells.

ANACREONTIC.

τὸ κάλλιστον μὲν ὕδωρ.—Pindar.

BLAME not the Bowl—the fruitful Bowl!
  Whence wit, and mirth, and music spring
And amber drops elysian roll,
  To bathe young Love's delighted wing.
What like the grape Osiris gives
  Makes rigid age so lithe of limb?
Illumines memory's tearful wave,
  And teaches drowning hope to swim?
Did Ocean from his radiant arms
  To earth another Venus give,
He ne'er could match the mellow charms
  That in the breathing beaker live.

Like burning thoughts which lovers hoard
  In characters that mock the sight,
Till some kind liquid, o'er them pour'd,
  Brings all their hidden warmth to light—
Are feelings bright, which, in the cup,
  Though graven deep, appear but dim,
Till fill'd with glowing Bacchus up,
  They sparkle on the foaming brim.
Each drop upon the first you pour
  Brings some new tender thought to life,
And as you fill it more and more,
  The last with fervid soul is rife.

The island fount, that kept of old
  Its fabled path beneath the sea,

And fresh, as first from earth it roll'd,
  From earth again rose joyously,
Bore not beneath the bitter brine
  Each flower upon its limpid tide
More faithfully than in bright wine
  Our hearts will toward each other glide.
Then drain the cup, and let thy soul
  Learn, as the draught delicious flies,
Like pearls in the Egyptian's bowl,
  Truth beaming at the bottom lies.

The Song of the Drowned.

DOWN, far down, in the waters deep,
  Where the booming surges above us sweep,
Our revels from night till morn we keep:
And though with us the cup goes round
Upon every shore where the blue waves sound,
Yet here, as it passes from lip to lip,
Alone is found true fellowship;
For only the dead, where'er they range,
'Tis the Dead alone who never change.

What boots your pledges, ye sons of Earth!
Or to whom ye drink in your hours of mirth,
When gather'd around your festal hearth?
Ye fill to love! and the toast ye give
Will hardly the fumes of your wine outlive!

To friendship fill! and its tale is told,
Almost ere the pledge on your lip grows cold!
For only the Dead, where'er they range,
'Tis the Dead alone who never change.

Then come, when the "bolt of death is hurl'd,"
Come down to us from that bleak, bleak world,
Where the wings of sorrow are never furl'd:
Come, and we'll drink to the shades of the past;
To the hopes that mock'd in life to the last;
To the lips and the eyes we once would adore,
And the loves that in death can delude no more!
For the Dead, the Dead, where'er they range,
'Tis only the Dead who never change.

No More—No More.

NO more—no more of song to-night;
  Oh, let no more thy music flow!
Those notes that once could wake delight,
Come o'er me like a spirit-blight,
A breathing of the faded past,
Whose freshest hopes to earth were cast
  Long, long ago.

A livelier strain! nay, play, instead,
  That movement wild and low,
That chanting for the early dead
Which best beseems spring's blossoms fled,

A requiem for each tender ray
That from life's morning stole away
Long, long ago.

Boat Song.

We court no gale with wooing sail,
We fear no squall a-brewing;
Seas smooth or rough, skies fair or bluff,
Alike our course pursuing.
For what to us are winds, when thus
Our merry boat is flying,
While, bold and free, with jocund glee,
Stout hearts her oars are plying!

At twilight dun, when red the sun
Far o'er the water flashes,
With buoyant song, our bark along
His crimson pathway dashes;
And when the night devours the light,
And shadows thicken o'er us,
The stars steal out, the skies about,
To dance to our bold chorus.

Sometimes, near shore, we ease our oar,
While beauty's sleep invading,
To watch the beam through her casement gleam,
As she wakes to our serenading;

Then, with the tide, we floating glide
  To music soft, receding,
Or drain one cup, to her fill'd up,
  For whom these notes are pleading.

Thus, on and on, till the night is gone
  And the garish dawn is breaking;
While landsmen sleep, we boatmen keep
  The soul of frolic waking;
And though cheerless then our craft look, when
  To her moorings day hath brought her,
By the moon amain she is launch'd again,
  To dance o'er the merry water.

Where dost thou Loiter, Spring?

WHERE dost thou loiter, Spring,
  Whilst it behoveth
Thee to cease wandering
  Where thy breeze roveth,
And to my lady bring
  The flowers she loveth?

Come with thy melting skies,
  Like her cheek, blushing,
Come with thy dewy eyes
  Where founts are gushing;
Come where the wild bee hies
  When dawn is flushing.

Lead her where, by the brook,
  The first blossom keepeth,
Where, in the shelter'd nook,
  The callow bud sleepeth,
Or with a timid look
  Through its leaves peepeth.

Lead her whereon the spray,
  Blithely carolling,
First birds their roundelay
  For my lady sing—
But keep, where'er she stray,
  True love blossoming.

CHANSONNETTE.

IT haunts me yet! that early dream
  Of first fond Love;
Like the ice that floats in a summer stream
  From frozen fount above,
Through my river of life 'twill drifting gleam,
  Wherever its waves may flow;
Flashing athwart each sunny hour
With a strangely bright but chilling power,
  Ever and ever to mock their tide
    With its illusive glow;
  A fragment of hopes that were petrified
    Long—long ago!

A Portrait.

NOT hers the charms which Laura's lover drew,
Or Titian's pencil on the canvas threw;
No soul enkindled beneath southern skies
Glow'd on her cheek and sparkled in her eyes;
No prurient charms set off her slender form
With swell voluptuous and with contour warm;
While each proportion was by Nature told
In maiden beauty's most bewitching mould.
High on her peerless brow—a radiant throne
Unmix'd with aught of earth—pale genius sat alone.
And yet at times within her eye there dwelt
Softness that would the sternest bosom melt,
A depth of tenderness which show'd, when woke,
That woman there as well as angel spoke.
Yet well that eye could flash resentment's rays,
Or, proudly scornful, check the boldest gaze;
Chill burning passion with a calm disdain,
Or with one glance rekindle it again.
Her mouth—oh! never fascination met
Near woman's lips half so alluring yet;
For round her mouth there play'd, at times, a smile,
Such as did man from Paradise beguile;
Such, could it light him through this world of pain,
As he'd not barter Eden to regain.
What though that smile might beam alike on all;
What though that glance on each as kindly fall;
What though you knew, while worshipping their power,
Your homage but the pastime of the hour?

Still they, however guarded were the heart,
Would every feeling from its fastness start—
Deceive one still, howe'er deceived before,
And make him wish thus to be cheated more,
Till, grown at last in such illusions gray,
Faith follow'd Hope, and stole with Love away.
Such was Alinda; such in her combined
Those charms which round our very nature wind;
Which, when together they in one conspire,
He who admires must love—who sees, admire.
Variably perilous; upon the sight
Now beam'd her beauty in resistless light,
And subtly now into the heart it stole,
And, ere it startled, occupied the whole.
'Twas well for her, that lovely mischief, well,
That she could not the pangs it waken'd tell;
That, like the princess in the fairy tale,
No soft emotions could her soul assail;
For Nature,—that Alinda should not feel
The wounds her eyes might make, but never heal,—
In mercy, while she did each gift impart
Of rarest excellence, *withheld a heart!*

Birthday Thoughts.

At twenty-five—at twenty-five,
 The heart should not be cold;
It still is young in deeds to strive,
 Though half life's tale be told;
And Fame should keep its youth alive,
 If Love would make it old.

But mine is like that plant which grew
 And wither'd in a night,
Which from the skies of midnight drew
 Its ripening and its blight—
Matured in Heaven's tears of dew,
 And faded ere her light.

Its hues, in sorrow's darkness born,
 In tears were foster'd first;
Its powers, from passion's frenzy drawn,
 In passion's gloom were nurs'd—
And perishing ere manhood's dawn,
 Did prematurely burst.

Yet all I've learnt from hours rife
 With painful brooding here
Is that, amid this mortal strife,
 The lapse of every year
But takes away a hope from life,
 And adds to death a fear.

BYRON.

HIS hopes would fade like sunset clouds,
  Which melt in blackening skies,
Until he sought that peace in crowds
  A cheerless home denies.

He roam'd, an Arab on life's waste,
  Its kindly springs to drink;
A TANTALUS, from whose hot taste
  The cooling waters shrink.

And when he would each trace forget
  That mark'd his early course,
Remembrance brought him but regret,
  Regret became remorse.

And then he watch'd life's lamps go out,
  Its friendships one by one
Decay, and leave his soul without
  A light beneath the sun.

THE THAW-KING.

HIS VISIT TO NEW YORK.

HE comes on the wings of the warm south-west,
  In the saffron hues of the sunbeam dress'd,
And lingers awhile on the placid bay,
As the ice-cakes languidly steal away,
To drink those gems which the wave turns up,
Like Egyptian pearls in the Roman's cup.

Then hies to the wharves where the hawser binds
The impatient ship from the wistful winds,
And slackens each rope till it hangs from on high,
Less firmly pencil'd against the sky:
And sports in the stiffen'd canvas there
Till its folds float out in the wooing air:
Then leaves these quellers of Ocean's pride
To swing from the pier on the lazy tide.

He reaches the Battery's grassy bed,
And the earth smokes out from beneath his tread;
And he turns him about to look wistfully back
On each charm that he leaves on his beautiful track;
Each islet of green which the bright waters fold,
Like emeralds, fresh from their bosom roll'd,
The sea just peering the headlands through
Where the sky is lost in its deeper blue,
And the thousand barks which securely sweep
With silvery wing round the land-lock'd deep.

He loiters awhile on the springy ground,
To watch the children gambol around,
And thinks it hard that a touch from him
Cannot make the aged as lithe of limb;
That he hath no power to melt the rime,
The stubborn frost, that is made by Time:
And sighing, he leaves the urchins to play,
And launches at last on the world of Broadway.

There were faces and figures of heavenly mould,
Of charms not yet by the poet told;

There were dancing plumes, there were mantles gay,
  Flowers and ribbons flaunting there,
Such as of old on a festival day
  The Idalian nymphs were wont to wear,
And the Thaw-king felt his cheek flush high,
  And his pulses flutter in every limb,
As he gazed on many a beaming eye,
And many a form that flitted by,
  With twinkling foot and ankle trim.

And he practiced many an idle freak,
  As he lounged the morning through ;
He sprung the frozen gutters aleak,
  For want of aught else to do ;
And left them, black as a libeller's ink,
To gurgle away to the sewer-sink.

He sees a beggar, gaunt and grim,
  Arouse a miser's choler,
And he laughs while he melts the soul of him
  To fling the wretch a dollar ;
And he thinks how small a heaven 'twould take
For a world of souls like his to make.

He read, placarded upon the wall,
"That the country now on its friends did call,
  For liberty was in danger ;"
And he went to a room ten feet by four,
Where a chairman and sec., and couple more
  (Making *five* with our friendly stranger),

By the aid of four slings and two tallow tapers,
Were preparing to tell in the morning papers
Of the UNION unbroken,
By this very token,
"That the people in mass last night had woken
And their will at the primal meetings spoken!"
And he trembled himself to the tip of his wing
At the juggling might of the *Caucus* king.

He saw an Oneida baskets peddling
Around the place where the polls were held;
And a Fed. the Red-skin kicked, for meddling,
As the Indian a Democrat's ballot spell'd.
That son of the soil
Who had no vote,
How dared he to spoil
A trick so neat,
Meant only to cheat
The voters who hither from Europe float!

And now as the night falls chill and gray,
Like a drizzling rain on a new-made tomb,
And his father, the Sun, has slunk away,
And left him alone to gas and gloom,
The Thaw-king steals in a vapor thin
Through the lighted porch of a house, wherein
Music and mirth were gayly mingled;
And groups like hues in one bright flower
Dazzled the Thaw-king while he singled
Some one on whom to try his power.

He enters first in a lady's eyes,
And thrusts at a dandy's heart;
But the vest that is made by *Frost* defies
The point of the Thaw-king's dart;
And the baffled spirit pettishly flies
On a pedant to try his art;
But his aim is equally foil'd by the dust-
Y lore that envelops the man of must.

And next he tries with a fiddler's sighs
To melt the heart of a belle;
But around her waist there's a stout arm placed,
Which shields that lady well.
And that waist! oh! that waist—it is one that you would
Like to clasp in a waltz, or—wherever you could.

Her figure was fashion'd tall and slim,
But with rounded bust and shapely limb;
And her queen-like step as she trod the floor,
And her look as she bridled in beauty's pride,
Was such as the Tyrian heroine wore
When she blush'd alone on the conscious shore,
The wandering Dardan's unwedded bride.

And the Thaw-king gazed on that lady bright,
With her form of love and her looks of light,
Till his spirits began to wane,
And his wits were put to rout;
And entering into a poet's brain,
He thaw'd these verses out:

"River, O river, thou rovest free
From the mountain height to the fresh blue sea,
Free thyself, while in silver chain
Linking each charm of land and main.
Calling at first thy banded waves
From hill-side thickets and fern-hid caves,
From the splinter'd crag thou leap'st below
Through leafy glades at will to flow—
Idling now with the dallying sedge,
Slumbering now by the steep's moss'd edge,
With statelier march once more to break
From wooded valley to breezy lake;
Yet all of these scenes, though fair they be,
River, O river, are bann'd to me!

"River, O river! upon thy tide
Gayly the freighted vessels glide;
Would that thou thus couldst bear away
The thoughts that burthen my weary day,
Or that I, from all, save thou, set free,
Though laden still, might rove with thee.
True that thy waves brief lifetime find,
And live at the will of the wanton wind—
True that thou seekest the ocean's flow
To be lost therein for evermoe!
Yet the slave who worships at glory's shrine,
But toils for a bubble as frail as thine,
But loses his freedom here, to be
Forgotten as soon as in death set free."

A Birthday Meditation.

ANOTHER year! alas, how swift,
  Alinda, do these years flit by,
Like shadows thrown by clouds that drift
  In flakes along a wintry sky.
Another year! another leaf
Is turn'd within life's volume brief,
And yet not one bright page appears
Of mine within that book of years.

There are some moments when I feel
  As if it should not yet be so;
As if the years that from me steal
  Had not a right alike to go,
And lose themselves in Time's dark sea,
Unbuoyed up by aught from me;
Aught that the future yet might claim
To rescue from their wreck a name.

But it was love that taught me rhyme,
  And it was thou that taught me love;
And if I in this idle chime
  Of words a useless sluggard prove,
It was thine eyes the habit nursed,
And in their light I learn'd it first,
It is thine eyes which, day by day,
Consume my time and heart away.

And often bitter thoughts arise
  Of what I've lost in loving thee,

And in my breast my spirit dies,
  The gloomy cloud around to see
Of baffled hopes and ruin'd powers
Of mind, and miserable hours—
Of self-upbraiding, and despair—
Of heart, too strong and fierce to bear.

"Why, what a peasant slave am I,"
  To bow my mind and bend my knee
To woman in idolatry,
  Who takes no thought of mine or me.
O God ! that I could breathe my life
On battle-plain in charging strife—
In one mad impulse pour my soul
Far beyond passion's base control.

Thus do my jarring thoughts revolve
  Their gather'd causes of offence,
Until I in my heart resolve
  To dash thine angel image thence ;
When some bright look, some accent kind,
Comes freshly in my heated mind,
And scares, like newly flushing day,
These brooding thoughts like owls away.

And then for hours and hours I muse
  On things that might, yet will not be,
Till one by one my feelings lose
  Their passionate intensity,
And steal away in visions soft,
Which on wild wing those feelings waft

Far, far beyond the drear domain
Of reason and her freezing reign.

And now again from their gay track
  I call, as I despondent sit,
Once more these truant fancies back
  Which round my brain so idly flit;
And some I treasure, some I blush
To own—and these I try to crush—
And some, too wild for reason's rein,
I loose in idle rhyme again.

And even thus my moments fly,
  And even thus my hours decay,
And even thus my years slip by,
  My life itself is wiled away;
But distant still the mounting hope,
The burning wish with men to cope
In aught that minds of iron mould
May do or dare for fame or gold.

Another year! another year,
  ALINDA, it shall not be so;
Both love and lays forswear I here,
  As I've forsworn thee long ago.
That name, which thou wouldst never share,
Proudly shall fame emblazon where
On pumps and corners posters stick it,
The highest on the JACKSON ticket.

THE YACHTER.

MY bark is my courser so gallant and brave;
Like a steed of the prairie she bounds o'er the wave,
And the breast of the billow, as onward I roam,
Swelling proudly to meet her, is fleck'd by her foam.

Like the winds which her canvas exultingly fill,
I float as I list, and I rove as I will;
The breeze cannot baffle, for with it I veer,
Or in the wind's eye like the petrel I steer.

O'er the pages of story the student may pore,
The trumpet the soldier may charm to the war,
In the forest the hunter his haven may see,
But the bounding blue water and shallop for me.

With no haven before me—beneath me my home—
All heaven around me wherever I roam,
I am free—I am free as the shrill piping gale
That whistles its music as onward I sail.

"BRUNT THE FIGHT."

SUGGESTED BY AN EMBALMED INDIAN HEAD.

NOT to the conflict, where those death wounds came
That still discolor thine undaunted brow,
Not to the wildwood, when thy soul of flame
Found vent alone in deeds—all nameless now,

Though startled fancy first by these is caught—
Not, not to these dost thou enchain my thought!

The tuft of honor, streaming there unshorn,*
The separate gashes, every one in front,
Prove knightly crest was ne'er more bravely borne
By charging champion through the battle's brunt,
While those old scars, from forays long since past,
Bespeak the warrior's life from first to last.

Bespeak the man who acted out the *whole*—
The whole of all he knew of high and true,
All that was vision'd in his savage soul,
All that his barbarous powers on earth could do;
Bespeak the being perfect to the plan
Of Nature when she moulded such a man.

His simple law of duty and of right—
Oneness of soul in action, thought and feeling;
His mind, disturb'd by no conflicting light,
His narrow faith, so clear in each revealing;
His will untrammell'd to act out the part
So plainly graved on his untutor'd heart:

Envy I these? Would I for these forego
The broader scope of being that is mine?
His bond of sense with spirit once to know
Would I the strife for truth and good resign?
How can I—when, *according to my light,*
My law, like his, is still to BRUNT THE FIGHT!

* See "Vigil of Faith," stanza xxii.

BUENA VISTA.

[Supposed to be written by a Mexican prisoner within the American lines at Saltillo.]

WE saw their watch-fires through the night
Light up the far horizon's verge;
We heard at dawn the gathering fight
Swell like the distant ocean surge—
The thunder-tramp of mountain hordes
From distance sweeps a boding sound,
As Aztec's twenty thousand swords
And clanking chargers shake the ground.

A gun!—now all is hushed again—
How strange that lull before the storm,
That fearful silence o'er the plain!—
Halt they their battle line to form?
It booms—it booms—it booms again,
And through each thick and thunderous shock
The war-scream seems to pierce the brain,
As charging squadrons interlock.
Columbia's sons—of different race—
Proud Aztec and bold Alleghan,
Are grappled there in death embrace,
To rend each other, man to man!

The storm-clouds lift,* and through the haze,
Dissolving in the noontide light,

* "While the battle was going on, there came up a thick black cloud, which extended itself across the valley immediately over the two armies, entirely concealing them from my

I see the sun of Aztec blaze
  Upon her banner broad and bright!
And on—still on, her ensigns wave,
  Flinging abroad each glorious fold;
While drooping round each sullen stave
  Cling Alleghan's but half unrolled.

But stay! that shout has stirred the air;
  I see the stripes—I see the stars—
O God! who leads the phalanx there
  Beneath those fearful meteor bars?
"Old Zack"—"Old Zack"—the war-cry rattles
  Amid those men of iron tread,
As rung "Old Fritz," in Europe's battles,
  When thus his host great Frederick led!
Like Cordillera's snow-fed flood
  Its torrent-track through forests rending,
Like Santiago's crashing wood
  Through which it whirls, in foam descending,
So Taylor's power in that wild hour
  Upon our central might is thrown,
So round his dread resistless tread
  Our bleeding ranks are rent and strewn.

Oh! hardly from that carnage dire
  We drag our patriot chief away—

view, from which I could hear peal after peal of heavy thunder, and see the sharp lightning descend. At the same time I could hear the roar of the cannon of both armies, then engaged in deadly conflict; as though Heaven's artillery was contending against that of feeble man."—*Letter from an Officer, in the Knickerbocker.*

Who, crushed by famine, steel and fire,
  Yet claims as his the desperate day!
That day whose sinking light is shed
  O'er Buena Vista's field, to tell
Where round the sleeping and the dead
  Stalks conquering TAYLOR'S sentinel.

My Dog.

AN ear that caught my slightest tone,
  In kindness or in anger spoken;
An eye that ever watch'd my own,
  In vigils death alone has broken;
Its changeless, ceaseless, and unbought
  Affection to the last revealing;
Beaming almost with human thought,
  And more—far more than human feeling!

Can such in endless sleep be chill'd,
  And mortal pride disdain to sorrow,
Because the pulse that here was still'd
  May wake to no immortal morrow?
Can faith, devotedness, and love,
  That seem to humbler creatures given
To tell us what we owe above,—
  The types of what is due to Heaven,—

Can these be with the things that *were*,
  Things cherish'd—but no more returning,

And leave behind no trace of care,
 No shade that speaks a moment's mourning?
Alas! my friend, of all of worth
 That years have stolen or years yet leave me,
I've never known so much on earth,
 But that the loss of thine must grieve me.

THE MINT JULEP.

ποτ' ἐγένετο θεοῖσι.

'TIS said that the gods on Olympus of old
 (And who the bright legend profanes with a doubt?)
One night, 'mid their revels, by Bacchus were told
 That his last butt of nectar had somehow run out!

But determined to send round the goblet once more,
 They sued to the fairer immortals for aid
In composing a draught which, till drinking were o'er,
 Should cast every wine ever drank in the shade.

Grave Ceres herself blithely yielded her corn,
 And the spirit that lives in each amber-hued grain,
And which first had its birth from the dew of the morn,
 Was taught to steal out in bright dew-drops again.

Pomona, whose choicest of fruits on the board
  Were scatter'd profusely in every one's reach,
When call'd on a tribute to cull from the hoard,
  Express'd the mild juice of the delicate peach.

The liquids were mingled while Venus look'd on
  With glances so fraught with sweet magical power,
That the honey of Hybla, e'en when they were gone,
  Has never been miss'd in the draught from that
    hour.

Flora, then, from her bosom of fragrancy, shook,
  And with roseate fingers press'd down in the bowl,
All dripping and fresh as it came from the brook,
  The herb whose aroma should flavor the whole.

The draught was delicious, and loud the acclaim,
  Though something seem'd wanting for all to be-
    wail,
But JULEPS the drink of immortals became,
  When JOVE himself added a handful of hail.

Notes on Kachesco.

NOTES ON KACHESCO.

PART I.—STANZA III.

Those peaks where fresh the Hudson takes
His tribute from an hundred lakes.

THE lakes which form the sources of the Hudson in the Adirondac wilderness are supposed to exceed this number. For a topographical account of this romantic region, see the first and second official reports of George E. Hoffman, Esq., "Chief Engineer for the Survey of the Upper Hudson and its Branches," to the Legislature of the State of New York, 1838–39. These mountains, when first visited by the present writer, in his college vacations, were much frequented by roving Indian hunters, who often showed a hunter's friendliness to his youngsterhood, and more than one of whom has since met with a violent death amid these solitudes. The country seemed, at that time, about to be settled by white people as a grazing district, but the opening of the Erie Canal, soon afterward, diverted emigration westward; and the Chief Engineer of the Upper Hudson speaks, in his first report, of former "clearings" and old roads being rendered impassable by a young and thick forest growth, and wild animals making their lair in the cabins of former settlers, who had migrated to the prairies.

Within the last five years, however, the publication of the Geological Survey of the State has again brought the whole Sacandaga and Adirondac region into fresh and favorable notice; and its rich mineral resources, not less than its magnificent scenery, are now the frequent themes of correspondence in our periodicals, alike by scientific and sporting tourists. These, since the first edition of this poem was published, have made its attractions pretty generally known; still the following summing up of its characteristics, which is copied here from the "Ithaca Chronicle," may be acceptable to the summer tourist, from the memorandum of different routes it offers to those who would penetrate the "little Switzerland" described in the text:

"An immense plateau of land, elevated more than fourteen hundred feet above tide, occupies a central position between the Canada line on the north and Mohawk River on the south, the Champlain valley on the east and Lake Ontario on the west. It covers an area of 8000 square miles, equal to the whole of Massachusetts and a corner of Rhode Island. The Adirondac Mountains are the crowning summits of the great uplift, and Tahawus or Marcy the monarch of the whole, his brow of rock just on the boundary of eternal frost. You enter this savage region by Lake Champlain to Westport or Keesville—or from the south more readily by Caldwell to Schroon Lake and Portersville, thence to Long Lake (*Incapahco*), or the Iron Works—or, lastly, from Saratoga by the way of the Sacandaga and Lake Pleasant to Raquet Lake. In this uninhabited territory are a hundred lakes of from one to twenty miles in length—some reposing in the perpetual shade of interlocking mountains, others flashing like silver mirrors in quiet valleys; and all of them alive with the finest fish. Streams unnumbered leap from the rocky flanks of lofty heights, and dash off oceanward beneath the foliage of a primeval forest. In these the speckled trout dart in shoals, and bound to the surface toward evening, as if in a perfect frolic. Through the mountain gorges stray the sullen bear and tawny moose, while the beautiful deer feeds along the margin of the solitary waters, and the panther screams in the tangled thicket. From Tahawus and Whiteface you can sweep a circle of 500 miles in circumference, and all an ocean of mountains, holding in their embrace nearly thirty visible lakes."

STANZA XIV.

And much he told of Metai lore,
Of Wabenos we call enchanters, etc.

ALGONQUIN MYTHOLOGY is rich in its native interpreters. Sorcery, as practiced by the Metai, Wabeno or Jossakeed of our aborigines, keeps them, in many tribes, more or less in bondage to a class of men who seem to officiate as conjurers, priests and soothsayers. Our Indians, although worshipping one Great Spirit, believe in the existence of a familiar spirit or δαίμων in all things (Lafitau, James, Schoolcraft); and in their lodge lore we have an interminable calendar of demi-gods and minor divinities, who keep the woods from being lonely (see Discourse on Indian Mythology, Coll. N. Y. Hist. Soc.). Of these divinities, Nabozhoo, Manabozhoo or Nanabushe (for all these names apply to the same mythological personage) and Pa-puckwis are the favorites among their story tellers. The writer has given the principal legend of the former in his "Wild Scenes of the Forest and Prairie" (Bentley, London, 1838). It is more curious than poetic.

With regard to PA-PUCKWIS, the red elf who figures in many a pleasant tale preserved in Schoolcraft's valuable "Algic Researches," he is always represented as very small, and as frequently being invisible, vanishing and reappearing to those whom he visits with his pranks. It is as the leader of the PUCKWUDJEES, however, that this godikin is most entitled to consideration. These elvish beings are described as inhabiting and loving rocky heights, caves, crevices or rural and romantic points of land, upon the lakes, bays and rivers, particularly if they be crowned with pine trees. They are depicted in the oral legends of the Algonquins as flitting among thickets, or running, with a whoop, up the sides of mountains and over plains. The following explanation, by our most distinguished Algonquin scholar, of the etymology of the term, may interest the philological reader:

"The term *puck*, as heard in Puckwudj, is found in a number of compound phrases in the Odjibiwa dialect of the Algonquins. It assumes an adjective, a verbal or a substantive form, according to the adjuncts which either precede or follow it, for the vocabulary of the language, although founded on roots which are generally monosyllables, is exceedingly compound in its structure. Thus, if the term *puck* be thrust in between the particles *pa* and *ewa*, it means a grasshopper; if between *pa* and *ewiss*, it is the name of a mythological personage who, in the lodge legends of the Algonquins, is a roving, jumping, dancing, adventure-hunting character—a kind of *harum-scarum* or merry-andrew, who performs all sorts of feats and pranks. If followed by the verbal particle *eta*, it means to strike, to beat, to belabor. If put between the vowel *a* and *wa*, it denotes a nodding flag or 'cat-tail.' If followed by the substantive term *emik*, it denotes a rampant beaver. Prefixed to the particle *wudj*, the result is an adjective phrase meaning wild, roving, unfixed, changing. *Ininee* is the diminutive form of the term for *man*. The most common interpretation of the word *Puck-wudj-ininee* is 'the little wild man of the woods that vanishes.'"—*Extract of a letter to the author from H. R. Schoolcraft, Esq., Dec.* 2, 1844.

With regard to "the Path of Spirits" and other matters relating to disembodied souls in the subsequent stanza, that excellent Indian authority, Dr. Edwin James, formerly of the army, gives us an Algonquin term for the milky way, which term he translates "the path of ghosts." The early French writers also set down the name of the galaxy in Iroquois as Ennoniawa, or "the path of souls." "An Indian (says James) of whom I made some inquiries respecting a friend of his that had recently died replied to me in a very earnest manner, '*kunkotow naiponit otachuk*,' 'at no time will die his shadow.'"

The same writer, when on duty at Prairie du Chien, heard some Indians reproving one of their tribe who had been ill for what they considered imprudent exertion and exposure during his recovery, telling him that "*his shadow was not yet well settled.*" Among the Chippewas, a covering of cedar bark is put over the top of the grave to shed the rain. This is roof-shaped, and the whole structure looks slightly like a house in miniature. It has gable-ends, and through one of these, at the head of the grave, a hole is cut. Mr. Schoolcraft once asked a Chippewa why this was done. "To allow the soul to pass out and in," said the Indian. "I thought (said Mr. S.) that you believed that the soul went up from the body, at the time of death, to a land of happiness. How, then, can it remain in the body?" "There are two souls," answered the Indian philosopher. "How can that be?" "It is easily explained," continued the Chippewa. "You know that in dreams we pass over wide countries, and see hills, and lakes, and mountains, and many scenes which pass our eyes and affect us; yet, at the same time, our bodies do not stir, and there is a soul left with the body, *else it would be dead!* So you perceive it must be another soul that accompanies us!"—*Oneota.* Lafitau, I think, has several authorities to show that this belief was shared by the Iroquois; and Le Pere de Brebœuf, writing nearly 200 years ago, tells that, having asked an old Huron why they called bodies which had been long dead by the name of E-kenn (a plural word signifying souls), he was answered that they believed all men to possess two souls, both divisible and material, yet both rational—that one separated itself from the body at death, yet remained in the cemetery until "the feast of the dead," when it was changed into a turtle-dove, or, as is more commonly believed, went directly to the place of spirits. The other soul is, as it were, attached to the body, and still possesses the corpse, remaining always in the grave, unless some one should reproduce it as an infant; and the proof of this last metamorphosis is found in the extraordinary resemblance which exists often between young persons and those who have long been dead. The catalogue of our aboriginal metamorphoses seems to be inexhaustible. (See Schoolcraft's writings, *passim.*) One of the most beautiful is that of Ojeeg, "*the Summer-Maker,*" who sprang from the top of a mountain against the sky, and after making a hole large enough to let the warm airs of summer rush through, for the benefit of his friends below, was himself changed into a constellation. More touching, however, are the transformations which follow death caused by the religious fast which public opinion compels the young warrior to keep when he first comes of age. This fast is often maintained by the pious aspirant who is unfavored with any visitation either from this world or the other until death closes the torture he endures without complaining; and many a fragile youth thus perishing from inanition, in this treble trial of his firmness, his faith and his fancy, has passed away less gracefully than Opee-chee, that gentle and famished boy whom his Manito changed into a robin as he sank exhausted when he had just half covered his bosom with the red war-paint.—*Gilman's* "*Life on the Lakes,*" 1837.

With regard to the worship of our aborigines, whether the Manitou of the Algonquin, the Neo, Owaneo or Hawaneyu of the Iroquois, or the Wacondah of the prairie tribes be its object, their priests seem to have little agency in ministering at the Indian's adoration of the Great Spirit. There are no witnesses save from the invisible world of his lonely act of forest worship, and his piety is the spontaneous, and, as we might say, the involuntary, tribute of his feelings (James). The recognition of the sun as at once the emblem and the eye of the Eternal, often dwelt upon by early Canadian travellers, among our northern tribes (Lafitau), is but seldom alluded to by modern observers, but the traditionary belief is still traceable in the usage of each pious smoker offering the first incense of his calumet to the sun, whence it was originally lighted (Picard). Tobacco, which those not reclaimed from heathen usages still insist is the choicest offering a devout Indian can make, either to the great Father of all or to his own special tutelary divinity, is believed in its human use to induce chastity and sober all the sensual appetites, and by thus purifying the soul to prepare it for visions of the spiritual world, and at the same time impel the seer to communicate with those around him (Lafitau)

Yet often will the hunter in his tribulation part with the last morsel of this specific for spirituality in himself in order to propitiate some testy spirit among the Manitoag that dulls his flint or damps his priming, or blows his canoe upon some rough headland he is trying to double in the tempest (Schoolcraft).

Among the Algonquins, Kitchi Manitou is the great good spirit of all, while MACHINETO (or Matchi Manito) represents the opposing evil spirit (James). Among the Iroquois we have NEO and KLUNEOLUX, corresponding in character with those divinities (Schoolcraft). But we find no tradition or doctrine showing that the fiend can torment the Red Man's spirit in another world. He passes through many trials on his way to paradise, but his only durable punishment is that of transformation into an inferior animal. Before the newly-departed shadow can reach those blessed islands amid which lie embowered the villages of the dead, many obstacles are to be encountered and many difficulties overcome. The disembodied shades must cross a river, too deep and rapid to be forded, in a stone canoe; they must next traverse a bottomless chasm bridged only by an enormous snake, on whose slimy back they walk; and finally pass over a still more boisterous torrent than the preceding upon a single tottering log, which spans the roaring gulf below. This log is constantly vibrating upward and downward with such violence that many, alike children and adults, are precipitated into the gulf, when they are changed into fish and turtles and other cold-blooded animals (Coll. N. Y. Hist. Soc.).

There are many traditions of once-departed spirits having repassed this perilous bridge and come back to earth. Dr. James has collected several legends of this kind; and in Picard's Ceremonies Religieuses is preserved an account nearly identical with the following story of an Iroquois Orpheus:

Driven almost to despair by the death of his sister, Sayadyio resolved to seek her in the world of spirits. His journey, long and painful, might have proved bootless throughout if he had not met with an aged man who encouraged his search, and at the same time gave him an empty calabash, in which he might enclose the soul of his sister, should he succeed in finding it. The same accommodating old gentleman likewise promised Sayadyio that he would give him also the maiden's brains, which he had in his possession, he being the appointed keeper of that portion of the dead. The young man arrived at last in the place of souls. The spirits were astonished to see him, and eagerly fled his presence. Tharonhiawagou, the master of the ceremonies in phantom good society, received him well, however, and became instantly his friend. At the moment of Sayadyio's arrival the souls were all gathered for a dance, according to their custom at that hour. He recognized his sister floating through the phantom corps de ballet, and rushed to embrace her, but she vanished like a dream of the night. Tharonhiawagou, however, kindly furnished our adventurer with a mystical rattle of strange musical power; and when the sound of the spirit-drum, which marks the time for the choral dance of those blessed shades, had summoned them back to their places, and the Indian flute poured the enchanting notes that lift them along upon a tide of melody, the magic rattle of Sayadyio, a stronger "medicine" than either, charmed the soul of the Indian maiden within the reach of her brother. Quick as light, Sayadyio dipped up the entranced spirit, and shut it securely in his calabash; then, despite the entreaties and artifices of the captive soul, who only thought of being delivered from her present prison, this Iroquois Orpheus made the best of his way back to earth, and arrived in safety with his precious charge in his native village. His own and his sister's friends were now called together, and the body of the damsel was disinterred and prepared to receive the soul which should reanimate it. Everything was ready to complete the resurrection, when the impatience of one of the female attendants utterly foiled the success of the attempt. Some red sister of Eve who was among the lookers on could not restrain her curiosity. She had loved the deceased maiden, and she must needs peep into the calabash to see how the soul looked divested of all drapery. Whereon, precisely as Eros of old spread his pinions and flew from prying Psyche, so the soul took wing on the instant, and fled from prying love. As the flying shade casts no shadow in its movements through our atmosphere, Sayadyio could not trace it even for a moment in its flight; and abandoning all pursuit, he was obliged to sit down disconsolate, with the conviction that he had derived no other benefit from his journey than that of having been in the place of souls, and having it in his power to relate certain true things which would not fail of reaching posterity.

STANZA XVI.

Of portages and lakes whose name
As uttered in his native speech,
If memory could have hoarded each,
A portage-labor 'twere to carry.

It is very difficult, even with the aid of the straggling Indians who still haunt the wilderness around the sources of the Hudson, to recover the aboriginal *terminology*. The Hurons, the Adirondacs, the Otawas and Iroquois had probably there, for centuries, their common hunting-ground; and the geographical names, therefore, often traceable to at least four different languages, are necessarily much confused; while, from occasional similarity of physical feature in lake and mountain, none but our habitual dwellers in these solitudes could properly identify the Indian terms with the localities to which they refer. Still, the explanation of those which occur in the succeeding stanzas may, perhaps, interest the idle tourist who wanders to the wild region described in the text: *Reuna* (or A-rey-una), Green-rocks, Paskungemah, better known perhaps as Tupper's Lake. *Onegora*, "wampum strewn," equivalent to the Seneca Tunessa-sah, "a place of pebbles." *Towarloondah* (Mohawk), "Hill of Storms;" supposed to be the "Mount Emmons" of the Geographical Survey. *Oukorlah* (Mohawk), "The Big Eye," from a singular white spot near the summit. It is named

"Mount Seward" in the Geological Survey. *Ounowarlah* (Mohawk), "Scalp Mountain." *Nodoneyo*, "Hill of the Wind Spirit." *Wahopartenie*, known also as "White Face Mountain." *Yowhayle*, "Dead-ground." *Tioratie* (Mohawk), "The Sky, or Sky-like." *Kurloonah*, "Place of the Death Song." *Cahogaronta*, "Torrent in the Woods." *Tahawus* means literally, "He splits the Sky;" it is called "Mount Marcy" in the Geological Survey. *Metauk*, "The Enchanted Wood," evidently from *Metai* and Awuk. *Sandanona*, a mountain near Lake Henderson. *Gwiendauqua*, a cascade, like "A Hanging Spear." *Twenungasko*, a double voice.

STANZA XVII.

Yes, INCA-PAH-CO! *though thy name*
Has never flowed in poet's numbers.

"Inca-pah-co" (*Anglice*, Lindenmere) is so called by the Indians from its forests of bass-wood, or American linden. It is better known perhaps by the insipid name of "Long Lake," and is one of that chain of mountain lakes which, though closely interlacing with the sources of the Hudson, discharge themselves through Racket River into the St. Lawrence. They lie on the borders of Essex, in Hamilton county, New York. Inca-pah-co, where the scene of our story is chiefly laid, is about eighteen miles in length; but though a noble lake, it is perhaps not so picturesque in character as some of those referred to in the previous note. The finest of all, perhaps, *Killoquore* (Mohawk), *rayed*, like the sun, is sometimes called "Ragged Lake."

STANZA XXVI.

"*. . . . that gorge's quaking throat,*
Reft by Otneyarh's giant band,
Where splinters of the mountain vast,
Though lashed by cable roots, aghast,
Toppling, amid their ruin, stand."

The Giant's Pass, near Lake Henderson, is one of the finest scenes of the Adirondac Mountains, if not one of the most extraordinary upon the continent. The writer has attempted a description of it in his "Wild Scenes of the Forest and Prairie," where a particular version of the Iroquois legend of Otneyarh, or the band of *Stonish Giants*, is also given. These fabled monsters were walking quarries of flint, in the shape of men who could stride through your common granite as if it were cheese. They certainly dashed the crags to the right and left after a most extraordinary fashion in that colossal "Notch" near the Adirondac Iron Works. See the testimony of Cusick, an Indian, about these ancient folk, in Schoolcraft's "Notes on the Iroquois."

PART II.—STANZA I.

Bright Nulkah, doe-eyed forest girl!

Nulkah, or "Noolka," means "doe-eyed," in one of our Indian dialects.

STANZA VIII.

The Red Bird's nest above it swung;
There often the Ma-ma-twa sung;
And Moning-gwuna's quills of gold
Through leaves like flickering sunshine told.

The Red Bird, Baltimore Oriole or "hanging bird," as he is often called from the mode of building his nest, is very brief in his visits to this mountain region. The Ma-ma-twa, or Cat-bird, the finest of our northern songsters, save the Bob-o-linkum, exercises his mocking freakishness there upon sounds which he can rarely find to imitate in the woods elsewhere; and this may make him linger longer with the short summer. But the Moning-gwuna, "High-Hold," "Golden Winged Woodpecker," and "Flicker," as he is severally called, seems to make this his favorite region; and wherever there is an opening in the forest, his rich orange-colored wing will be seen playing, like bright-hued flowers, around some old gray stump.

STANZA XXII.

To wander thus where'er he may,
Of woman and of man the scorn.

In some tribes, when the penalty of death is thus changed for that of degradation, the criminal who so regains his forfeited life is considered as *unsexed.* He then becomes the mental slave of the first person who chooses to take possession of him, and is obliged to submit to tasks of exposure the most toilsome, and domestic offices the most humiliating; his master or owner (or *husband,* as he is whimsically called) being permitted to exercise every species of tyrannical cruelty upon him, provided he shed not the blood of the poor wretch who is thus subjected to his caprices. See Tanner's Narrative; see also "The Equawish," in "*Life on the Lakes,*" by the author of "*Legends of a Log Cabin.*"

SELECTED LIST OF BOOKS

PUBLISHED BY

PORTER & COATES,

No. 822 Chestnut Street,

PHILADELPHIA.

The Books in this List, unless otherwise specified, are bound in Cloth.

☞ All of our Publications mailed, post-paid, on receipt of price. ☜

SELECTED LIST OF BOOKS

PUBLISHED BY

PORTER & COATES,

No. 822 Chestnut Street,

PHILADELPHIA.

ALEXANDER WILSON AND CHARLES LUCIEN BONAPARTE.

AMERICAN ORNITHOLOGY; OR, THE NATURAL HISTORY OF THE BIRDS OF THE UNITED STATES. Illustrated with Plates engraved and colored from original Drawings taken from Nature. By ALEXANDER WILSON. With a life of the author, by GEORGE ORD, F.R.S. With Continuation, by CHARLES LUCIEN BONAPARTE (Prince of Musignano). 3 vols., imperial 8vo., with a folio volume of carefully colored plates embracing nearly 400 figures of birds mostly life size. Elegantly bound in cloth, extra gilt top, $97.00; half Turkey morocco, gilt edges, $110.00.

THE SAME, complete in 5 vols., 3 of letter-press and 2 vols. quarto of plates. Cloth, extra, gilt top, $97.00; half Turkey, gilt edges, $110.00.

A new and magnificent edition of this world-renowned work, printed from new stereotype plates, on the finest laid paper, and bound in the best manner. The plates are printed from the original plates, engraved by Lawson, "the first ornithological engraver of our age," and are carefully colored, after the author's own copies. The superiority of this work for accuracy of description and naturalness of drawing, has long been acknowledged. Daniel Webster speaks of it in the highest terms, saying that of the salt water birds, mentioned in Wilson, "he had shot every one, and compared them with his delineations and descriptions, and IN EVERY CASE found them PERFECTLY ACCURATE TO NATURE." And the *London Quarterly Review* characterized it as "an admirable work, unequaled by any publication in the old world, for accurate delineations and just description." A moment's comparison of this work with any other on the same subject, will convince the most skeptical of its great superiority. One of its chief values being, that the birds are mostly of the size of life, enabling any one to easily recognize them in nature; and, at the low price it is now offered, should be in every public and private library of any pretentions.

"With an enthusiasm never excelled, this extraordinary man penetrated through the vast territories of the United States, undeterred by forests or swamps, for the sole purpose of describing the native birds."—*Lord Brougham, Architecture of Birds.*

"Wilson contemplated nature as she really is, not as she is represented in books: he sought her in her sanctuaries;—the shore, the mountain, the forest, were alternately his study, and there he drank the pure stream of knowledge at the fountain head."—*Swainson.*

"With regard to the literary merit of his American Ornithology, passages occur in the prefaces and descriptions which, for elegance of language, graceful ease, and graphic power, can scarcely be surpassed."—*Encyclopedia Brittanica, Vol. XXI.*

EDWARD GIBBON.

THE DECLINE AND FALL OF THE ROMAN EMPIRE. With Notes by Rev. H. H. Milman. To which is added a complete Index. 6 vols. crown 8vo, with a steel portrait. Cloth, extra, per set, $9.00; sheep, library style, per set, $10.50; half calf, gilt, per set, $18.00.

"Gibbon, the architect of a bridge over the dark gulf which separates ancient from modern times, whose vivid genius has tinged with brilliant colors the greatest historical work in existence."—*Alison.*

DAVID HUME.

THE HISTORY OF ENGLAND, FROM THE INVASION OF JULIUS CÆSAR TO THE ABDICATION OF JAMES THE SECOND, 1688. A new Edition, with the author's last corrections and improvements. To which is prefixed a short account of his life, written by himself. With steel portrait. 6 vols. crown 8vo, cloth, extra, per set, $9.00; sheep, library style, per set, $10.50; half calf, gilt, per set, $18.00.

"Considered as a calm and philosophic narrative, the history of Hume will remain as a standard model for every future age. His just and profound reflections, the inimitable clearness and impartiality with which he has summed up the arguments on both sides on the most momentous questions which have agitated England, as well as the general simplicity, uniform clearness, and occasional pathos of his story, must for ever command the admiration of mankind. In vain we are told that he is often inaccurate, sometimes partial; in vain are successive attacks published on detached parts of his narrative, by party zeal or antiquarian research: his reputation is undiminished: successive editions issuing from the press attest the continued sale of his work; and it continues its majestic course through the sea of time, like a mighty three-decker, which never even condescends to notice the javelins darted at its sides, from the hostile canoes which from time to time seek to impede its progress."—*Alison's Essays.*

THOMAS BABINGTON MACAULAY.

THE HISTORY OF ENGLAND FROM THE ACCESSION OF JAMES II. Standard Edition, with an Index. 5 vols. crown 8vo, with a steel portrait. Cloth, extra, per set, $7.50; sheep, library style, per set, $8.75; half calf, gilt, $15.00.

"With the rest of the world, we come with our homage to Macaulay. Steady, strong and uniform, the stream of his thought continues to flow: and, without effort, or without outward sign of it, he keeps his place as the first living (1856) writer of English prose. * * * On whatever side we look at this book, whether the style of it or the matter of it, is alike astonishing. The style is faultlessly luminous: every word is in its right place; every sentence is exquisitely balanced; the current never flags. Homer, according to the Roman poet, may be sometimes languid; Mr. Macaulay is always bright, sparkling, attractive."—*Westminster Review*, April, 1856.

DUCHESS OF ORLEANS.

MEMOIR OF THE DUCHESS OF ORLEANS. By the MARQUESS DE H——, together with Biographical Souvenirs and Original Letters. Translated from the French, by Prof. G. H. DE SCHUBERT. One volume, with a portrait on steel, 12mo, pp. 391. $1.50.

"The materials of this volume consist of a memoir by the Marquis de H——, which is an interesting narrative of the varied and peculiar fortunes of the subject, and a collection of souvenirs and original letters by Professor Schubert, of Germany, who was the family tutor of the Duchess of Orleans. The work derives not a little interest from the character of the Duchess, which was equally remarkable for loveliness and heroism, especially during her troubled career after the abdication of Louis Philippe. The translation shows fidelity and considerable skill, and will be regarded as a valuable accession to biographical reading."—*Harper's Magazine.*

SIR WALTER SCOTT.

WAVERLEY NOVELS. Complete in 23 vols. Illustrated. Toned paper. Price per vol., *Globe Edition:* cloth, extra, $1.25; half calf, gilt, $2.75. *Standard Library Edition:* cloth, extra, gilt tops, bev. boards, $1.50; half calf, gilt, $3.00; half mor., gilt tops, $3.50.

Waverley.
Guy Mannering.
Antiquary.
Rob Roy.
Black Dwarf, and Old Mortality.
Heart of Mid Lothian.
Bride of Lammermoor, and A Legend of Montrose.
Ivanhoe.
Monastery.
Abbot.
Kenilworth.
Pirate.
Fortunes of Nigel.
Peveril of the Peak
Quentin Durward.
St. Ronan's Well.
Redgauntlet.
The Betrothed, and the Talisman.
Woodstock.
Fair Maid of Perth.
Anne of Geierstein.
Count Robert of Paris, and Castle Dangerous.
Chronicles of the Canongate.

This is the best edition for the library or for general use published. Its convenient size, the extreme legibility of the type, which is larger than is used in any other edition, either English or American, its spirited illustrations, quality of the paper and binding, and the general execution of the presswork, must commend it at once to every one.

TALES OF A GRANDFATHER. Uniform with the "Waverley Novels." Illustrated. 4 vols. Toned paper. Price per vol., *Globe Edition:* cloth extra, $1.25; half calf, gilt, $2.75. *Standard Library Edition:* cloth extra, gilt tops, bev. boards, $1.50; half morocco, gilt tops, $3.00; half calf, gilt, $3.50.

The only edition containing the Fourth Series, "Tales from French History."

IVANHOE. A Romance. Youth's Favorite Edition. Illustrated. Crown 8vo. $1.50.

LADY OF THE LAKE. With twenty-five engravings on wood, from designs by Birket Foster and John Gilbert. 16mo. Bev. boards, $1.50; half calf, gilt, $3.00; full Turkey mor. antique, $4.00.

LIFE OF SIR WALTER SCOTT, with remarks upon his Writings, by Francis Turner Palgrave; an Essay on Scott, by David Masson, M.A., and Dryburgh Abbey; a Poem, by Charles Swain. With fine portrait on steel, 12mo. Illuminated cover, 30 cents. cloth, extra, 60 cents.

"Relates the events in the life of the illustrious novelist in an agreeable style, with an unpretending, but singularly acute, criticism of his writings."—*New York Tribune.*

"A centennial offering of large worth. The biography is brief but comprehensive, while the remarks upon his writings which crop out every here and there, are marked by great judgment and keen appreciation."—*Philadelphia Inquirer.*

"One of the ablest reviews of Scott's life and works that has ever been written. It is very able and very just."—*New York Evening Mail.*

THE BEAUTIES OF WAVERLEY. Selections of the most striking passages from the Waverley Novels. With forty-five fine steel engravings. Elegantly printed on fine paper, and bound in the most tasty style. A new and perennial gift book. One volume, crown 8vo. Cloth, full gilt, extra, $5.00; morocco, bevelled boards, antique, $8.00.

RUFUS W. GRISWOLD, D.D.

THE PROSE WRITERS OF AMERICA. With a Survey of the Intellectual History, Condition, and Prospects of the Country. New edition, thoroughly revised and completed to the present time, with a supplementary Essay on the Present Intellectual Condition and Prospects of the Country. By Prof. JOHN H. DILLINGHAM, A.M. With seven portraits on steel and vignette title. Imperial 8vo. Cloth, extra, gilt top, bevelled boards, $5.00; sheep, marbled edges, library style, $6.00; half calf, $7.50; full Turkey morocco, $10.00.

"We are glad to possess, in this form, portions of many authors whose entire works we should never own, and if we did should probably never find time to read. We confess our obligations to the author for the personal information concerning them which he has collected in the memoirs prefixed to their writings. These are written in a manner creditable to the research, ability, and kindness of the author."—*William Cullen Bryant.*

"An important and interesting contribution to our national literature. The range of authors is very wide; the biographical notices full and interesting. I am surprised that the author has been able to collect so many particulars in this way. The selections appear to me to be made with discrimination, and the criticisms show a sound taste and a correct appreciation of the qualities of the writers, as well as I can judge."—*William H. Prescott, the Historian.*

"Can be cordially recommended for its sterling qualities, and the handsome style in which it has been gotten up by the publishers makes it particularly worthy of the notice of those who wish to make a Christmas present that will be appreciated by the recipient."—*Philadelphia Evening Telegraph.*

"Is really a desirable acquisition to any library, and, indeed, a library could scarcely be called complete without it."—*Marshall (Mich.) Times.*

GEMS FROM THE AMERICAN POETS. With brief biographical notices. With a fine engraving on steel. 32mo, cloth, 60 cents; illuminated sides, 90 cents; Turkey mor., extra, $1.50.

FREDERIC H. HEDGE, D.D.

THE PROSE WRITERS OF GERMANY. With Introductions, Biographical Notices, and Translations. With six portraits on steel and engraved title. Imperial 8vo. Cloth, extra, gilt top, bevelled boards, $5.00; sheep, marbled edges, library style, $6.00; half calf, gilt, $7.50; full Turkey morocco, $10.00.

"There is no book accessible to the English or American reader which can furnish so comprehensive and symmetrical a view of German literature to the unitiated: and those already conversant with some of the German classics will find here valuable and edifying extracts from works to which very few in this country can gain access."—*Prof. A. P. Peabody, in North American Review.*

"It is universally recognised as one of the best collections of specimens of German literature in the English language. It has been prepared on the plan of giving a limited selection of authors, with large extracts from their works. The translations from the editor's own pen are singularly vigorous, and in the accomplishment of his task, he has had the co-operation of several American scholars."—*New York Tribune.*

"A new and beautiful edition of a work of sterling merit. Compilations are good even in our own language, for so great is the multitude of books that few have leisure to read a tithe of them. But to the great stores of literature in foreign tongues, only those skilled in them have access. The treasures of German literature are inaccessible to most American readers. It is, therefore, no common addition to our information and pleasure, to have put before us well selected passages of the best works of the most celebrated German authors. This is done with the most excellent judgment in this volume. The reader of it will here form some acquaintance with the principal German classics, and that acquaintance he may improve by a further perusal of those which he finds most to his taste. Enough, however, s given to furnish an ample specimen of the style and method of each writer. Many complete pieces are furnished. Among those to whom considerable space is accorded, are Kant, Lessing, Herder, Goethe, Schiller, the Schlegels, Richter, Heine; with these are many others of celebrity."—*Age, Philadelphia.*

HENRY WADSWORTH LONGFELLOW.

THE POETS AND POETRY OF EUROPE. A New and Revised Edition, with the addition of 137 pages of entirely new matter, *never before published*, making it one of the most elegant and complete works extant. With Introduction, Biographical Notices, and Translations, from the earliest period to the present time. By Prof. HENRY WADSWORTH LONGFELLOW. Illustrated with engravings on steel and engraved title. Imperial 8vo. Cloth, extra gilt top, beveled boards, $6; sheep, marbled edges, library style, $7.50; half calf, gilt, $9; Turkey morocco, $12.

"In all this there is great clearness and precision; the details dear to the student of a particular literature or literary epoch, but, confusing to the average culture, are sacrificed to the fullness with which the principal and important features are brought out. Whenever it is possible, the criticism is founded upon the opinions of each writer's countrymen, and in all cases it appears to us that the best authorities are consulted; and one of the best is Mr. Longfellow himself, who speaks his own mind only too sparingly. His work is often merely that of an editor, but he does it with that taste, sympathy and good sense, which his whole literary life embodies in such degree, that we feel anything else to be impossible with him, and gives it thus the finest value of original production. The labor involved in the preparation of such a volume as this, will by no means appear to the general reader it delights, and to whom we venture to suggest grateful consideration of the vast acquaintance with authors and authorities, the tacit service of comparison and selection implied by the abundance and the succinctness with which every topic is treated. We will not say that here is all the general reader need know of the poets and poetry of Europe, but we assure him that he cannot do better than possess himself of all the information here given, and that he could no where else find it so availably and so agreeably presented, and with so little that he need not know. To this new edition Mr. Longfellow has added a supplement of 137 pages, devoted to such poets as have recently won distinction, and to the poets whom recent study has brought into notice anew. The poems in this supplement are marked by that greater fidelity and regard to the originals which no one has done half so much to urge upon translators as Mr. Longfellow himself, in the high example of his 'Dante.' Here are his own exquisite translations from German, French, Italian, and Spanish; here is one version, most sympathetically tender and spirited, by Mr. Lowell; here is a part of Faust in Bayard Taylor's conscientious and admirable English; here are some songs from Heine, by Leland; here are Mrs. Wister's charming pieces from De Musset; here are Bryant's Specimens of modern Spanish poetry; here are Rosetti's beautiful versions from the earliest Italian poets, and here are abundant extracts from the latest. The supplement, in fact, lays before the reader the freshest and best poetry of all Europe, and worthily completes the work. It is not easy to give a just idea of its merits and graces, but those who already know it will not need a lecture from us upon it, and to those who do not we can but heartily commend it."—*Atlantic Monthly, January*, 1871.

"This edition has been revised and enlarged by the author, and contains his best touches and corrections to his labors. But they have stood the test of criticism. Their accuracy and felicity have been acknowledged by the best scholars in Europe. The attainments of Mr. Longfellow as a linguist have been recognized by those best qualified to judge them in each sphere of his labors. . . . In it is given, in a convenient form, a summary of the poetic literature of Europe which is not to be found elsewhere."—*The Age, Philadelphia.*

"It is now a better book than ever, the Professor having added an appendix and supplement, the latter dated 1870, containing a very precious list of newer poetical translations. . . . The supplement is very choice and interesting, and absolutely rejuvenates the work. Here we have specimens from Bayard Taylor's translation of Faust, not yet received in complete book form, a charming passage from King Rene's Daughter, &c., &c. The whole volume is an acquisition to our letters, and to that disposition of literary curiosity, an honorable distinction of the American people, which has made such a difficult work, so well done, necessary."—*The Evening Bulletin, Philadelphia.*

DEAN STANLEY.

SERMONS PREACHED during his Tour in the East. With Notices of some of the Localities visited. Published by arrangement with the author. New edition. With plan and diagram. 12mo, cloth extra, $1.50.

Dean Stanley's Sermons are famous, as finished specimens of pulpit oratory, and the fourteen comprised in this volume are pre-eminently characteristic of their distinguished author. They are specially interesting for the very graphic description of the various localities visited during the tour in the course of which they were delivered.

Three of these sermons were preached in Egypt, on the Nile, and in the great hall of the Temple of Karnak; four were preached in Palestine, in the harbor of Jaffa, at Jacob's Well, at Nazareth, and by the Sea of Galilee; three more were preached in Syria, on Mt. Hermon, in the Temple of Baalbec, and under the cedars of Lebanon; three were preached upon the Mediterranean, with the fresh impressions of Ephesus, Patmos, and Malta, &c. These circumstances of composition and delivery would give interest even to ordinary discourses. But these are not ordinary. The thought is simple, but very free and very wide. It is not merely illustrative of the scenes and the history, but it is excellent counsel, both practical and spiritual, to the principal listeners."—*North American Review for July*, 1863.

REV. TREADWELL WALDEN.

THE HISTORY OF OUR ENGLISH BIBLE AND ITS SEVEN ANCESTORS. An Historical Plea for Revision. 16mo, tinted paper. Cloth extra, $1.25.

"In itself a story of profound interest, the ripe and elegant scholarship of the author gives it many additional charms; and it is specially welcome now, when our version of the Holy Book is to take another step forward, and assume that additional completeness necessary for a new age."—*Christian Union* (*Rev. Henry Ward Beecher, Editor*).

"We cordially commend it to the attention of our students and ministers, as a summary of useful and highly interesting information, even if they do not agree with the author on every point."—*United Presbyterian, Pittsburgh.*

"In this neatly printed little volume, Mr. Walden has gathered information concerning our English Bible, which everybody ought to possess, but which is not easy of access."—*Old School Presbyterian, St. Louis.*

"The book is extremely interesting, and will not fail to carry fresh information to very many readers."—*Watchman and Reflector* (*Baptist*).

"The work exhibits great research and scholarship, and is written in a clear and graceful style."—*Lutheran Observer.*

"A very Christian and scholarly effort."—*Methodist Protestant, Baltimore.*

"An admirable popular account of the successive steps in the growth of the English version of the Bible, from the first attempt by Wickliffe down to the final revision in the reign of King James."—*Sunday-School Times.*

THOMAS A'KEMPIS.

OF THE IMITATION OF CHRIST. Four books. New Edition, beautifully printed on toned paper. 18mo, cloth, extra, 50 cts.; cloth, extra, beveled boards, red edges, gilt stamp on side, 75 cents; cloth, extra, beveled boards, gilt edges, gilt stamp on side, $1.00; full Turkey morocco, antique, gilt edges, $2.50; full calf, antique, $2.50.

WILLIAM SHAKSPEARE.

COMPLETE WORKS. Dramatic and Poetical, with the "Epistle Dedicatorie," and the Address prefixed to the edition of 1623, a Sketch of the Life of the Poet, by ALEXANDER CHALMERS, A.M., and Glossarial and other Notes and References. Edited by GEORGE LONG DUYCKINK. With nine full-page steel Illustrations, a superb portrait on steel, from the celebrated Droeshout picture, and beautiful engraved title, on steel. 976 pages. Imperial 8vo. Cloth, extra, gilt back, $3.75; sheep, library style, $4.50.

FINE EDITION OF THE ABOVE, on extra calendered paper, with the addition of a History of the Early Drama and Stage to the time of Shakspeare, a full and comprehensive Life, by J. PAYNE COLLIER, A.M., Shakspeare's Will, critical and historical Introductions to each play, and thirty-five full-page tinted engravings, from designs by Nicholson, a superb portrait on steel from the celebrated Droeshout picture, and beautiful engraved title on steel. Imperial 8vo. 1084 pages. Half calf, gilt, $8.75; full Turkey morocco, $10.00.

POEMS AND SONNETS. With a fine engraving on steel. 32mo. Cloth, 60 cts.; illuminated side, 90 cts.; Turkey morocco, $1.50.

THOMAS PERCY, D.D., Bishop of Dromore.

RELIQUES OF ANCIENT ENGLISH POETRY: consisting of Old Heroic Ballads, Songs, and other pieces of the earlier poets, with some of later date, not included in any other edition. To which is now added a Supplement of many Curious Historical and Narrative Ballads, reprinted from rare copies, with a copious glossary and notes. New edition, uniform with the above. 558 pp. Imperial 8vo. Two steel plates. Fine cloth, bev. bds., gilt, $3.75; sheep, library style, $4.50; full Turkey morocco, $10.00.

"But, above all, I then first became acquainted with Bishop Percy's Reliques of Ancient Poetry. . . . . I remember well the spot where I read these volumes for the first time. It was beneath a huge plantanus tree, in the ruins of what had been intended for an old-fashioned arbor, in the *garden* I have mentioned. The summer day sped around so fast, that notwithstanding the sharp appetite of thirteen, I forgot the hour of dinner, was sought for with anxiety, and was still found entranced in my intellectual banquet. To read and to remember was in this instance the same thing, and henceforth I overwhelmed my schoolfellows, and all who would hearken to me, with tragical recitations from the ballads of Bishop Percy. The first time I could scrape a few shillings together, which were not common occurrences with me, I bought unto myself a copy of these beloved volumes, nor do I believe I ever read a book half so frequently, or with half the enthusiasm."—*Memoirs of his early Life, by Sir Walter Scott prefixed to Lockhart's Life of Scott.*

LORD BYRON.

COMPLETE WORKS. Prose and Poetry. With five engravings on steel. Imp. 8vo. Sheep, library style, $4.50; Turkey morocco, antique, $10.00.

"If the finest poetry be that which leaves the deepest impression on the minds of its readers,—and this is not the worst test of its excellence,—Lord Byron, we think, must be allowed to take precedence of all his distinguished contemporaries. 'Words that breathe, and thoughts that burn,' are not merely ornaments, but the common staple of his poetry; and he is not inspired or impressive only in some happy passages, but through the whole body and tissue of his composition."—*Lord Jeffrey, Edinburgh Review.*

THE MORAL AND BEAUTIFUL IN THE POEMS OF LORD BYRON. Edited by REV. WALTER COLTON. 32mo. Cloth, 60 cts.; illuminated side, 90 cts.; Turkey morocco, $1.50.

THOMAS HOOD.

COMPLETE WORKS. Prose and Poetry. Illustrated. 5 vols., crown 8vo, tinted paper. Cloth, extra, per vol., $1.75; half calf, gilt, per vol., $3.50; half morocco, antique, per vol., $3.25.

"This very good edition of a favorite author has the advantage of being lower in price and neater in appearance than any other yet published in this country."—*The Press, Philadelphia.*

POETICAL WORKS. 2 vols., crown 8vo, tinted paper. Cloth, extra, per vol., $1.75; half calf, gilt, per vol., $3.50; half morocco, gilt top, per vol., $3.50.

SELECT POETICAL WORKS. With a fine engraving on steel. 32mo. Cloth, 60 cents; illuminated side, 90 cents; Turkey morocco, $1.50.

"Hood's verse, whether serious or comic,—whether serene, like a cloudless autumn evening, or sparkling with puns like a frosty January midnight with stars,—was ever pregnant with materials for thought. . . . . Like every author distinguished for true comic humor, there was a deep vein of melancholy pathos running through his mirth; and even when his sun shone brightly, its light seemed often reflected as if only over the rim of a cloud.—*D. M. Moir.*

UP THE RHINE. Crown 8vo, tinted paper. Cloth, extra, $1.75; half calf, gilt, $3.50; half morocco, antique, $3.25.

HOOD'S COMICALITIES. A Series of Comical Pictures from Hood. Containing 200 illustrations, by Thomas Hood. Fully equal to Leech's and Cruikshank's admirable drawings. Oblong quarto. Half morocco, extra, $4.00.

JOHN MILTON.

COMPLETE WORKS. Standard Edition. With a Life of the Author, by Rev. John Mitford. 2 vols., crown 8vo, laid and tinted paper, largest type, $4.00. Library edition, with engravings on steel, 1 vol., 8vo, sheep, library style, $4.50; Turkey morocco, antique, $10.00.

ROBERT BURNS.

COTTER'S SATURDAY NIGHT. Elegantly illustrated with fifty engravings from drawings by Chapman. Engraved by Filmer. Beautifully printed by Ashmead, on the finest tinted plate paper. 4to, cloth extra, bev. boards, $4.50; Turkey morocco, antique, $9.00.

This noblest poem of "the greatest poet that ever sprang from the bosom of the people" until the issue of this edition had never been detached from the collected works of Burns, to receive the adornments of art which have been so bountifully and lovingly bestowed on Gray's "Elegy," Goldsmith's "Deserted Village," Coleridge's "Ancient Mariner," Thomson's "Seasons," and other kindred treasures of English verse. The poem itself is a classic, and the beauty and appropriateness of the illustrations to be found in this edition, place it far ahead of any other.

EDWARD, EARL OF DERBY.

THE ILIAD OF HOMER RENDERED INTO ENGLISH BLANK VERSE. From the ninth London edition, with all the author's latest revisions and corrections. With a Biographical Sketch of Lord Derby, by R. SHELTON MACKENZIE, D.C.L., LL.D. Two volumes, crown 8vo, on laid and tinted paper, gilt top, beveled boards, cloth extra, $4.00.

"It must equally be considered a splendid performance; and for the present we have no hesitation in saying that it is by far the best representation of Homer's Iliad in the English language."—*London Times.*

"The merits of Lord Derby's translation may be summed up it one word; it is eminently attractive; it is instinct with life; it may be read with fervent interest; it is immeasurably nearer than Pope to the text of the original. . . . It will not only be read, but read over again and again. . . . . Lord Derby has given to England a version far more closely allied to the original, and superior to any that has yet been attempted in the blank verse of our language."—*Edinburg Review.*

"As often as we return from even the best of them (other translations) to the translation before us, we find ourselves in a purer atmosphere of taste. We find more spirit, more tact in avoiding either trivial or conceited phrases, and, altogether, a presence of merits, and an absence of defects, which continues, as we read, to lengthen more and more the distance between Lord Derby and the foremost of his competitors."—*London Quarterly Review.*

"While the versification of Lord Derby is such as Pope himself would have admired, his Iliad is in all other essentials superior to that of his great rival. It is the Iliad we would place in the hands of English readers as the truest counterpart of the original, the nearest existing approach to a reproduction of that original's matchless feature."—*London Saturday Review.*

REV. JOHN KEBLE.

THE CHRISTIAN YEAR: Thoughts in verse for the Sundays and Holidays throughout the Year. 16mo, Cloth, red line, beautifully printed, $1.50; Turkey morocco, antique, gilt edges, $3.50.

"In this volume old Herbert would have recognized a kindred spirit, and Walton would have gone on a pilgrimage to make acquaintance with the author."—*London Quarterly Review.*

"These and many other thoughts and feelings concerning the 'vision and the faculty divine,' when employed on divine subjects, have arisen in our hearts, on reading—which we have often done with delight—The Christian Year, so full of Christian poetry of the purest character. Mr. Keble is a poet whom Cowper himself would have loved; for in him piety inspires genius, and fancy and feeling are celestialized by religion. We peruse his book in a tone and temper of spirit similar to that which is breathed on us by some calm day in spring, when

'Heaven and earth do make one imagery,'

and all that imagery is serene and still,—cheerful in the main, yet with a touch and tinge of melancholy which makes all the blended bliss and beauty at once more endearing and profound. We should no more think of criticizing such poetry than criticizing the clear blue skies, the soft green earth, the 'liquid lapse' of an unpolluted stream, that

'Doth make sweet music with the enamell'd stones,
Giving a gentle kiss to every flower
It overtaketh on its pilgrimage.'

Beauty is there,—purity and peace: as we look and listen we partake of the universal calm, and feel in nature the presence of Him from whom it emanated."—*Recreations of Christopher North, (John Wilson).*

CHARLES FENNO HOFFMAN.

COMPLETE POETICAL WORKS. Edited by his nephew, EDWARD FENNO HOFFMAN. New Library Edition, containing several poems never before published. With a new portrait on steel by Whitechurch, from a painting by Inman. Beautifully printed on laid and tinted paper. 16mo, cloth, extra, beveled boards, gilt top, $1.75.

CUMMINGTON, MASS., Aug. 5, 1873.

MY DEAR SIR:—I congratulate you on the completion of the task which you have undertaken of collecting the poetical productions of your uncle, Charles Fenno Hoffman, whom, while he lived in New York, I was proud to reckon among my friends, and whose kindly and generous temper and genial manners won the attachment of all who knew him. His poems bear the impress of his noble character. They are the thoughts of a man of eminent poetic sensibilities, who delights to sing of whatever moves the human heart—the domestic affections, patriotic reminiscences, the traditions of ancient loves and wars, and the ties of nature and friendship. These thoughts are expressed in musical versification with the embellishments of a ready fancy. The friends of your uncle have reason to thank you for presenting them in this manner the moral and intellectual image of him whom they have had such reason to esteem.

I am, sir, very truly yours,

WM. CULLEN BRYANT.

MRS. ELIZABETH F. ELLET.

PIONEER WOMEN OF THE WEST. One volume, 12mo, pp. 434. Illustrated, cloth extra, $1.50.

The history of the wives and mothers who ventured into the Western wilds, and bore their part in the struggles and labors of the early pioneers, is sketched in this work. The materials were collected from the records of private families, and the recollections of individuals who passed through the experiences of frontier and forest life. Descriptions of the domestic life and manners of the pioneers, and illustrative anecdotes, have been woven into the memoirs of prominent women, and notice has been taken of such political events as had an influence on the condition of the country.

"The biographies contain fine descriptions, enlivened with anecdotes of the domestic life and manners of those pioneer matrons, and are worthy of a perusal."—*The Watchman and Reflector* (*Baptist*).

"This volume is devoted to the history of the wives and mothers who bore a part in the struggles of the early pioneers in the Western wilds. Mrs. Ellet is familiar with this branch of the American annals. She has given much time to research on this subject. Her inquiries have been attended with remarkable success. Gathering a rich fund of local anecdote and tradition, furnished with interesting details by the descendants and the acquaintances of her subjects, and in many cases visiting the scenes of their adventures, she has obtained abundant materials for an attractive work, and has wrought them up with evident ability and good taste. Her volume, though full of interest to all classes of readers, is especially adapted for circulation at the Great West."—*Harper's Magazine.*

AGNES STRICKLAND.

STORIES FROM HISTORY. 12mo, illustrated, cloth extra, black and gold. Price, $1.25.

TRUE STORIES FROM ANCIENT HISTORY. Chronologically arranged from the Creation of the World to the Death of Charlemagne. 12mo, illustrated, cloth extra, black and gold. $1.25.

STORIES FROM MODERN HISTORY. 12mo, illustrated, cloth extra, black and gold. $1.25.

STORIES FROM ENGLISH HISTORY. 12mo, illustrated, cloth extra, black and gold. $1.25.

"Miss Strickland has performed her task with taste and ability."—*London Atheneum.*

THE LEADERS OF FRANCE; OR, THE MEN OF THE THIRD REPUBLIC. Biographical, Historical and Character Sketches. 12mo, satin cloth, black and gold, $1.75.

CONTENTS.—M. Thiers; Marshal MacMahon; M. Gambetta; M. Grevy; M. Barthelemy St. Hilaire; M. Rouher; The Duc de Broglie; M. Dufaure; M. Alexandre Dumas; The Duc D'Audiffret Pasquier; M. Ernest Picard; General Faidherbe; Bishop Dupanloup; M. Louis Veuillot; The Duc D'Aumale; M. Emile de Girardin; Father Hyacinthe; M. M. Erckmann-Chatrian; M. Henri Rochefort; M. Edmond About; M. Casimir Perier; M. Jules Simon; M. Victorien Sardou; Admiral Pothuau; M. Louis Blanc; M. Victor Hugo.

"These essays are the work of no 'prentice hand. They show not only a mastery of analytic and picturesque description, but an intimate acquaintance with the literature, the politics, and even the gossip of France and England during the past half century. * * * * Whoever wants instruction in the living politics and letters of France, cannot get it under a more rational or fascinating tutor than the unknown author of *The Men of the Third Republic*."—*The Christian Union, N. Y.*

"A collected republication of the very brilliant and well informed sketches which excited much attention and speculation on their appearance in the *Daily News*, and led men to ask whether there could be on the English press two men with opportunity and ability like those of the author of "The Member for Paris." Here are five-and-twenty sketches of notabilities who, since Sedan, have been prominent in French affairs, from M. Thiers and Jules Simon to Alexandre Dumas, Louis Blanc, and Victor Hugo; while the account of such less-known politicians as Gambetta, Grevy, Rouher, Dufaure, Rochefort, Girardin, will be interesting from the freshness of their information. Such brilliant and sagacious sketches as those of Thiers, Louis Blanc, and Jules Simon will be read very eagerly. So with the characterizations of literary celebrities like Dumas, M. M. Erckmann-Chatrian, Edmond About, and Victor Hugo. The charm and value of most of these sketches are, that they are histories as well as portraits. It argues well for France that novels like those of M. M. Erckmann-Chatrian are superseding those of Dumas and Paul DeKock, and penetrating every village."—*British Quarterly Review* (*the highest authority in England*).

Rev. WM. BACON STEVENS, Bishop of Penna.

SUNDAY AT HOME. A Manual of Home Service, intended for those who are occasionally hindered from attending the House of God. With Sermons and a Selection of Hymns. 12mo, cloth, extra, $1.50; cloth, extra, beveled boards, red edges, $2.00.

HOUSEHOLD WORSHIP. Partly responsive. A book of Family Prayers. By a Layman With an Introduction by REV. DANIEL MARCH, author of "Night Scenes in the Bible," &c. 12mo, cloth, extra, $1.25; cloth, extra, beveled boards, red edges, $1.75.

JOHN BUNYAN.

THE PILGRIM'S PROGRESS, FROM THIS WORLD TO THAT WHICH IS TO COME. With four beautiful illustrations, printed in colors. Large type. 16mo. Cloth, extra, $1.25; morocco, $3.00; Turkey, antique, $4.00.

"There is no book in our literature on which we could so readily stake the fame of the old unpolluted English language; no book which shows so well how rich that language is in its own proper wealth, and how little it has been improved by all that it has borrowed. . . . . We are not afraid to say that, though there were many clever men in England during the latter half of the seventeenth century, there were only two great creative minds. One of these minds produced the Paradise Lost, the other, the Pilgrim's Progress."—*Lord Macaulay.*

JANE R. SOMMERS.

HEAVENWARD LED; or, The Two Bequests. 12mo, paper, $1.25. Cloth extra, $1.75.

"It is really an excellent work."—*Germantown Telegraph.*

"This story is one of good society, is graphically told, and a sound moral is inculcated."—*Rutland Herald.*

"Artless in style and simple in plot, it is a pure and beautiful story, and richly merits a place in every Sunday-school library in the country."—*Toledo Commercial.*

"After a careful perusal we strongly recommend the work as one worthy of a place on the centre-table of every Christian family in the land. The story is well written, couched in beautiful language, and shows how much good may be done by those who take an interest in religious matters."—*Banner of the Church, Atlanta, Ga.*

LOUIS ENAULT.

THE PUPIL OF THE LEGION OF HONOR. Translated from the French by Mrs. Charles Pendleton Tutt. 8vo, paper, $1.00; cloth, $1.50.

"This is a translation from the French of a very fresh, quietly written, and interesting story, as unlike the average modern French novel as any thing can well be. There is perhaps somewhat more sentiment than Americans will care for, but the skill with which the story is told will more than atone for that."—*San Francisco Daily Record.*

"A very clear and natural, though rather un-Gallican story. A novel without a hero, unless M. De Verteins, who puts in a tardy appearance in time to marry Jeanne Derville, say at page one hundred and fifty, or thereabouts, it is a remarkably fresh, vivid story, nevertheless—the more vivid, perhaps, from the fact that, with the exception of Miss Derville herself, who is a sort of female John Halifax, it is not at all overwrought, and has none of the spectacularity so common in modern Gallic romance. Biographical in tone, and written in the manner of 'John Halifax,' it details the struggles of a young girl, Miss Derville, with exceeding minuteness, and considerable subjective power. The translation is well executed."—*Home Journal, New York.*

OLIVER GOLDSMITH.

THE DESERTED VILLAGE. A Poem. Exquisitely illustrated with thirty designs by George Thomas and Birket Foster. Elegantly printed in square 16mo, on the finest calendered paper. Cloth, gilt, extra, $1.50; morocco, antique, gilt edges, $2.50.

"There is no poem in the English language more universally popular than the Deserted Village. Its best passages are learned in youth, and never quit the memory."—*Chambers's Encyclopedia of English Literature.*

"'The Deserted Village' has an endearing locality, and introduces us to beings with whom the imagination contracts an intimate friendship. Fiction in poetry is not the reverse of truth, but her soft and enchanted resemblance; and this ideal beauty of nature has been seldom united with so much sober fidelity, as in the groups and scenery of the 'Deserted Village.'"—*Thomas Campbell.*

GEORGE CRUIKSHANK.

THE LOVING BALLAD OF LORD BATEMAN. Humorously illustrated by George Cruikshank. Sq. 16mo, boards, 25 cents.

YE BOOK OF SENSE. A new comic book. A companion to Book of Nonsense. With thirty-two illustrations. Oblong 8vo, boards, 50 cents; cloth, with plates colored, gilt, $1.00.

CHARLES KNIGHT.

HALF HOURS WITH THE BEST AUTHORS. With Short Biographical and Critical Notices. Elegantly printed on the finest paper. With fine steel portraits. 6 vols., crown 8vo. cloth, bev. boards, gilt tops, $9.00; half calf, gilt, $18.00; half morocco, gilt tops, $18,00; or bound in 3 vols., thick crown 8vo, fine English cloth, bev. boards, gilt tops, per set, $7.50; half calf, gilt, $12.00.

Selecting some choice passage of the best standard authors, of sufficient length to occupy half an hour in its perusal, there is here food for thought for every day in the year; so that if the purchaser will devote but one half-hour each day to its appropriate selection, he will read through these six volumes in one year, and in such a leisurely manner that the noblest thoughts of many of the greatest minds will be firmly implanted in his mind forever. For every Sunday there is a suitable selection from some of the most eminent writers in sacred literature. We venture to say, if the editor's idea is carried out, the reader will possess more information and a better knowledge of the English classics at the end of the year than he would by five years of desultory reading. The *variety* of reading is so great that no one will ever tire of these volumes. It is a library in itself.

MISS JANE PORTER.

The two following are new stereotype editions, in large, clear type, with initial letters, head and tail pieces, &c. The illustrations were designed expressly for this edition, and engraved in the highest style of art.

THE SCOTTISH CHIEFS. Illustrated by F. O. C. Darley. Crown 8vo, 748 pp. Fine English cloth, gilt. Price, $1.50; half calf, gilt, $3.50.

"Sir Walter Scott, in a conversation with King George IV, in the library at Carlton House, admitted that 'The Scottish Chiefs' suggested his 'Waverly Novels.'"—*Allibone's Dictionary of Authors.*

"This is a new and by far the best edition of a national romance which has been as much read and admired as almost any of Scott s or Dickens' novels. It is low-priced, well printed, and handsomely bound. Thousands of readers will be glad to go over this stirring tale once more."—*Philadelphia Press.*

REGINA MARIA ROCHE.

THE CHILDREN OF THE ABBEY. Illustrated by F. O. C. DARLEY. Uniform with "The Scottish Chiefs." Crown 8vo, 646 pp. Fine English cloth, gilt. Price, $1.50; half calf, gilt, $3.50.

"This classic is more neatly published in the new edition than we have ever seen it. It was long a standard, and had more favor than 'Thaddeus of Warsaw,' and it deserved better. It takes a new lease of existence now, and we almost envy those who read it for the first time."—*North American*, Philadelphia.

ROBERT McCLURE, M.D., V.S.

THE AMERICAN GENTLEMAN'S STABLE GUIDE. Containing a Familiar Description of the American Stable; the most approved Method of Feeding, Grooming, and General Management of Horses; together with Directions for the Care of Carriages, Harness, &c. Expressly adapted for the owners of equipages and fine horses. Cloth extra, illustrated. $1.50.

A handy manual, giving to the owner of a horse just the information of a practical nature that he often feels the need of, and by an author who thoroughly understands what he is writing about, and what is needed by every gentleman.

"Such a treatise has been needed for years, and we think this volume will supply the want. The illustrations are very good and timely."—*Pittsburgh Daily Gazette.*

JOHN J. THOMAS.

THE AMERICAN FRUIT CULTURIST. Containing Practical Directions for the Propagation and Culture of Fruit Trees in the Nursery, Orchard, and Garden. With Descriptions of the Principal American and Foreign Varieties cultivated in the United States. Second edition. Illustrated with 480 accurate figures. Crown 8vo. Cloth extra, bev. bds., gilt back. $3.00.

We have read hundreds of criticisms on this book, and they unanimously pronounce it the most *thorough, practical,* and *comprehensive* work published. The engravings are not copies of old cuts from other books, but are mainly original with the author.

J. H. WALSH, F.R.C.S. ("Stonehenge.")

THE HORSE IN THE STABLE AND THE FIELD; his Management in Health and Disease. From the last London edition, with copious Notes and Additions, by ROBERT MCCLURE, M.D., V.S., author of "Diseases in the American Stable, Field, and Farm-yard," with an Essay on the American Trotting Horse, and suggestions on the Breeding and Training of Trotters, by ELLWOOD HARVEY, M.D. With 80 engravings, and full-page engravings from photographs from life. Crown 8vo. Cloth, extra, bev. bds. $2.50.

"This Americanizing of 'Stonehenge' gives us the best piece of Horse Literature of the season. Old horsemen need not be told who 'Stonehenge' is in the British Books, or that he is the highest authority in turf and veterinary affairs. Add to these the labors of such American writers as Dr. McClure and Dr. Harvey, with new portraits of some of our most popular living horses, and we have a book that no American horseman can afford to be without."—*Ohio Farmer*, Cleveland, April 24, 1869.

"It sustains its claim to be the only work which has brought together in a single volume, and in clear, concise, and comprehensive language, adequate information on the various subjects of which it treats."—*Harper's Magazine*, July, 1869.

THADDEUS NORRIS.

AMERICAN FISH CULTURE. Giving all the details of Artificial Breeding and Rearing of Trout, Salmon, Shad, and other Fishes. 12mo, illustrated. $1.75.

"'Norris's American Fish Culture' published in this city by Porter & Coates, is passing around the world as a standard. Mr. Norris's authority will be quoted beside the tributaries of the Ganges, as already by those of the Hudson, the Humber, and the Thames. The English publishers of the book are Sampson Low, Son & Co.; and a late number of the *Athenæum*, after an attentive review of Mr. Norris's methods, concludes thus: 'Mr. Norris has rendered good service to the important subject of fish-culture by the present publication; and, although his book goes over ground (or water rather) occupied to a great extent by English writers on fish culture, it contains several particulars respecting this art as practised in the United States, which are valuable, and may be turned to profitable account by our pisciculturists.'"—*Philadelphia Evening Bulletin.*

THE AMERICAN ANGLER'S BOOK. Embracing the Natural History of Sporting Fish, and the Art of Taking Them. With Instructions in Fly Fishing, Fly Making, and Rod Making; and Directions for Fish Breeding. To which is added Dies Piscatoriæ; describing noted fishing places, and the pleasure of solitary fly fishing. New edition, with a supplement, containing a Description of Salmon Rivers, Inland Trout Fishing, &c. Illustrated with eighty engravings. 8vo, cloth extra. $5.50.

"Mr. Norris has produced the best book on Angling that has been published in our time. If other authors would follow Mr. Norris's example, and not write upon a subject until they had practically mastered it, we should have fewer and better works. *His* volume will live. It is thoroughly instructive, good-tempered, and genial."—*Philadelphia Press.*

HIRAM WOODRUFF.

HIRAM WOODRUFF ON THE TROTTING-HORSE OF AMERICA: HOW TO TRAIN AND DRIVE HIM. With Reminiscences of the Trotting-Turf. The Results of the Author's Forty Years' Experience and Unequalled Skill in Training and Driving, together with a Store of Interesting Matter concerning Celebrated American Horses. Edited by CHARLES J. FOSTER, of "Wilkes's Spirit of the Times." New edition, with Supplement, bringing it down to 1873. Illustrated with Steel-plate portrait of HIRAM WOODRUFF, and full page engravings from Photographs from Life, and Sketches of "Lady Thorne," "Goldsmith Maid," "Mac," "Flora Temple," &c., &c. 12mo, cloth, extra, $2.25; half calf, gilt, $4.00.

"The estimation in which we hold it is well known to our readers. We believe it to be *the most practical and instructive book that ever was published concerning the trotting horse;* and those who own or take care of horses of other descriptions may buy and read it with a great deal of profit."—*Wilkes's Spirit of the Times.*

"Hiram Woodruff was the great trainer of his day; but, by his unsullied integrity and unequalled capacity, he rose above his profession. No man could ever say of him that he had his price. Indeed, it is the universal testimony of all who knew him,—friends and foes,—that his integrity was absolutely unassailable. *It is a book for which every man who owns a horse ought to subscribe. The information which it contains is worth ten times its cost.*" —*Mr. Bonner's New York Ledger.*

"*This is a masterly treatise by the master of his profession,*—the ripened product of forty years' experience in handling, training, riding, and driving the trotting horse. There is no book like it in any language on the subject of which it treats. It is accepted as authority by the owners of racing trotters, and of fast roadsters. Its publication has been hailed by gentlemen as critically appreciative as Robert Bonner, and by trainers and drivers as distinguished as Sam Hoagland, Dan Mace, and Dan Pfifer. The book is unquestionably one of great value. For in America and England the development of the horse has long been considered second only in importance to the development of man. This work contains the results of forty years' uninterrupted labor in bringing the trotter up to the highest speed and greatest endurance of which he is capable. Before we read it we had seen with curious surprise very hearty commendation of it and eulogy of its author in the leading Presbyterian, Baptist, and Methodist journals. No wonder, for Hiram Woodruff's system is based on the law of love."—*New York Tribune.*

"We have a decided distaste for everything connected with horse-racing, and when the "Trotting Horse of America" was put into our hands the book dropped of its own weight on to the table. Ashamed of this prejudice, we took it up, and soon found ourselves reading at full pace about the way colts should be raised, and horses trained, and racers cared for, and the breed improved. . . . . In reading the book we were struck with the analogy between the scientific treatment of the horse and the best treatment of the human being. . . . . What a pity parents and teachers would not learn wisdom from the horse-trainer!"—*The (N. Y.) Liberal Christian (Unitarian).*

"One may read and study this book with profit, for it was written by a man who loved the horse, knew his peculiarities, and from the experience of years utters words of wisdom as to the best way of training and driving the noblest animal ever given to man for service. *The advice, the suggestions, the rules given in the book are invaluable.* If we owned a "stable," we would make our grooms study it; if we were a Vermont farmer, each son should have a copy, for, while it is specially devoted to trotting horses, the work contains valuable information for every man who owns or drives a horse."—*Boston Watchman and Reflector, (Baptist).*

"The record of his experience and suggestions constitutes, therefore, a valuable accession to our knowledge, and will prove to be of *standard authority among the most skilful.* The graphic style of his descriptions, the vivid pictures he draws of the breeding and education of his favorites, and the reminiscences he recalls of incidents on the turf, form a work of great merit. . . . Those who are desirous to form an accurate idea of the characteristics of the trotting horse, for their benefit as riders or drivers, *cannot find any other work in our language so replete with useful information,* interesting hints, and readable anecdotes. Hiram Woodruff is now dead, and it will be many a year before we shall look upon his equal in his line of business."—*The Nation.*

THE INSTRUCTIVE GAME OF MYTHOLOGY, with descriptive and biographical sketches on every card. Price, 50 cents.

THE INSTRUCTIVE GAME OF POPULAR QUOTATIONS, with descriptive, biographical and character sketches on every card. Price, 50 cents.

These games are uniform with "The Instructive Games of Authors and Poets," brought out last year. They are printed on the finest card-board, with colored backs, and are put up in either a handsome cloth case or a beautifully illuminated case as desired.

J. R. SYPHER.

THE YOUNG AMERICA SPEAKER. Designed for the use of the younger classes in Schools, Lyceums, Temperance Societies, &c. Containing selections in Prose, Poetry and Dialogue; in style, sentiment and expression, suited to the minds and spirits of the youth of the present day. 16mo, half bound, 75 cents.

"This little volume contains unexceptional selections of Prose, Poetry and Dialogue. The selections evidence extensive reading, good taste, and some experience with the predelictions of young declaimers."—*New Orleans Picayune.*

"An important and interesting addition to our school literature. The pieces presented in the work are well selected, and they have this advantage—each piece is short, and will not too seriously strain the faculties of any student. Being short, a greater variety is presented than in most speakers now before the public."—*Banner of the Church, Atlanta, Ga.*

THE AMERICAN POPULAR SPEAKER. Designed for the use of Schools, Lyceums, Temperance Societies, &c., &c. 12mo, half bound, 384 pp., $1.50.

"Admirably adapted to the purposes of declamation. We recognize many of the old standard pieces which boys have declaimed since our remembrance, with many also which we have not found in other similar compilations. The book is not encumbered with a multiplicity of rules and directions which serve to confuse and hinder the students rather than to help them; but a few, simple, practical directions are given which are admirable, and all that are needed. We commend the volume to the attention of teachers and students as one of high merit."—*Portland Evening Argus.*

"Excellent selections of prose and poetry and dialogues. The subjects embrace every conceivable want for school declamations with concise practical instructions for the speaker."—*New Bedford Evening Standard.*

MME. MARIE SOPHIE SCHWARTZ.

THE SON OF THE ORGAN GRINDER. A Novel. Translated from the Swedish by SELMA BORG and MARIE A. BROWN. With a portrait and sketch of Mme. Schwartz. 1 vol., 12mo. Cloth, $1.50; paper, $1.

This volume recommences the publication of the works of this brilliant and popular writer, and is considered equal to the best of her works yet translated.

MME. EMILE DE GIRARDIN, MM. THEOPHILE GAUTIER, JULES SANDEAU, and MERY.

THE CROSS OF BERNY; OR, IRENE'S LOVERS. A Novel. Translated from the French. 1 vol., 12mo. Cloth, $1.50; paper, $1.

"The Cross of Berny" is a brilliant literary tourney of four famous writers, and is pronounced by a former literary editor of *The Christian Union* to be the most powerful, witty, and interesting foreign novel translated since "On the Heights."

HENRY T. COATES.

THE COMPREHENSIVE SPEAKER. Designed for the use of Schools, Academies, Lyceums, &c. Carefully selected from the best authors, with Notes. Large 12mo, 672 pages, half bound, cloth sides, $1.75.

PHILADELPHIA, *April* 18, 1872.

I consider your "Comprehensive Speaker" to be one of the most valuable contributions to the literary apparatus of schools, academies, and lyceums ever published. But its usefulness is not limited to these institutions: it is an excellent family-table book, and should be in every private as well as in every public collection.

In carrying your readers through various departments of literature, from "gay to grave, from lively to severe," you have evinced much taste and judgment, as well as great industry. That the sale of so good a book should be large I should be sorry to doubt.

S. AUSTIN ALLIBONE,
Author of Allibone's Dictionary of Authors.

'It contains a judicious selection of pieces from the best authors, omitting all of doubtful morality, of a sectarian or political character, and of transient literary value. Great care has been taken in the selection of extracts to give the genuine text of the author without the errors in quotation and punctuation which are such a frequent blemish in this class of school books. A large proportion of the contents are from American authors, furnishing the materials for a comparative survey of our native literature."—*The New York Daily Tribune.*

"It is an excellent selection of pieces for declamation and reading."—*The Nation, New York.*

"On careful examination, we do not hesitate to characterize it as the BEST compilation of its class that has ever come under our notice. The merits of this large and varied collection are numerous. Hackneyed pieces have been carefully excluded, and political and sectarian pieces are not to be found in its pages. There are, of course, some humorous passages, in prose and verse, but none that are immoral or vulgar."—*The Philadelphia Press.*

"We cannot too highly commend the felicitous manner in which the compiler has accomplished his work. It is valuable as a volume for general reading as well. It seems to us wholly good, with nothing to add or change —a difficult achievement in view of the number of "Speakers" already in existence."—*Ohio State Journal, Columbus, Ohio.*

"The instructions are simple and practical, most admirably adapted to the student's use. Mr. Coates has shown in the preparation of this work a wide range of scholarship and rare good taste. The book is worthy of a grand success."—*Watchman and Reflector, Boston, (Baptist).*

"We need only say of this book that it is a remarkably rich collection of excerpts from the very best specimens of English prose and poetry, selected with singularly good taste and judgment. Its influence, as a familiar school-book, cannot be but very elevating."—*The Advance, Chicago.*

THE LATEST AND MOST IMPROVED GAMES.

THE INSTRUCTIVE GAME OF AUTHORS. Containing on each card the leading characters in the books named, the history of the author or the leading events mentioned in the books named, thus familiarizing one with each writer, by attracting the attention to some special persons or prominent incidents. Also, containing short biographical notices, in handsome cloth case. 50 cents.

THE INSTRUCTIVE GAME OF POETS. Uniform with the above in style. Cloth case. 50 cents.

JAMES HOGG, the Ettrick Shepherd.

THE MOUNTAIN BARD AND FOREST MINSTREL. Legendary Songs and Ballads. With two fine engravings on steel. 32mo, cloth, 60 cents; illuminated side, 90 cents; Turkey mor., $1.50.

"He is a poet, in the highest acceptation of the name."—*Lord Jeffrey.*

PERCY BYSSHE SHELLEY.

POETICAL WORKS. With a fine engraving on steel. 32mo, cloth, 60 cents; illuminated side, 90 cents; Turkey mor., $1.50.

ROBERT BLOOMFIELD.

THE FARMER'S BOY, and other Poems. Illustrated with a fine engraving on steel. 32mo, cloth, 60 cents; illuminated side, 90 cents; Turkey morocco, $1.50.

"Few compositions in the English language have been so generally admired as the Farmer's Boy. Those who agreed in but little else in literary matters, were unanimous in the commendation of the poetical powers displayed by the peasant and journeyman mechanic."—*Allibone's Dictionary Authors.*

ROBERT BURNS.

POETICAL WORKS. With a fine engraving on steel. 32mo, cloth, 60 cents; illuminated side, 90 cents; Turkey mor., $1.50.

"Burns is by far the greatest poet that ever sprang from the bosom of the people, and lived and died in an humble condition. Indeed, no country in the world but Scotland could have produced such a man; and he will be forever regarded as the glorious representative of the genius of his country. He was born a poet if ever man was."—*Prof. Wilson's Essay on Burns.*

WILLIAM DODD, LL.D.

THE BEAUTIES OF SHAKSPEARE. From the last London edition, with large additions, and the author's latest corrections. With two fine engravings on steel. Fine edition, on toned paper, with carmine border. Square 24mo. Cloth, gilt edges, $1.50; Turkey, $3.00; 32mo, cloth, 60 cts.; illuminated side, 90 cts.; Turkey morocco, $1.50.

This republication of a book so universally and deservedly popular as Dodd's Beauties, makes it peculiarly valuable as a gift book.

THOMAS HOOD.

POETICAL WORKS. With a fine engraving on steel. 32mo. Cloth, 60 cts.; illuminated side, 90 cts.; Turkey morocco, $1.50.

"Hood's verse, whether serious or comic,—whether serene, like a cloudless autumn evening, or sparkling with puns like a frosty January midnight with stars,—was ever pregnant with materials for thought. . . . . Like every author distinguished for true comic humor, there was a deep vein of melancholy pathos running through his mirth; and even when his sun shone brightly, its light seemed often reflected as if only over the rim of a cloud.—*D. M. Moir.*

THOMAS MOORE.

THE MORAL AND BEAUTIFUL FROM THE POEMS OF. Edited by REV. WALTER COLTON, author of "Deck and Port," &c., &c. With a fine engraving on steel. 32mo. Cloth, 60 cts.; illuminated sides, 90 cts.; Turkey morocco, $1.50.

"The combinations of his wit are wonderful. Quick, subtle, and varied, ever suggesting new thoughts or images, or unexpected turns of expression—now drawing resources from classical literature or of the ancient fathers—now diving into the human heart, and now skimming the fields of fancy—the wit or imagination of Moore (for they are compounded together), is a true Ariel, 'a creature of the elements,' that is ever buoyant and full of life and spirit."—*Chambers's Eng. Lit.*

ALFRED HOWARD.

THE BEAUTIES OF CHESTERFIELD. Consisting of Selections from the Works of Lord Chesterfield. 18mo, illustrated. Cloth extra, black and gold, $1.25.

CHARLES CALEB COLTON.

LACON; or, Many Things in Few Words Addressed to Those Who Think. Revised edition, with a life of the author. Globe edition, 16mo, cloth extra, $1.25.

"It is one of the most excellent collections of apothegms in the language."—*Allibone's Dictionary of Authors.*

COL. GEORGE CHESNEY.

THE BATTLE OF DORKING, AND GERMAN CONQUEST OF ENGLAND IN 1875; or, Reminiscences of a Volunteer. By an Eyewitness, in 1925. Reprinted from Blackwood's Magazine. 12mo, 64 pp., 30 cents; cloth, 50 cents.

"Everybody is talking about it, and everybody is quite right. We do not know that we ever saw anything better in any magazine, or any better example of the *vraisemblance* which a skilled artist can produce by a variety of minute touches. * * * * The writer of this paper, living about 1925, gives his son an account of his adventures as a Volunteer during the invasion of England fifty years before, and so powerful is the narrative, so intensely real the impression it produces, that the coolest disbeliever in panics cannot read it without a flush of annoyance, or close it without the thought that after all, as the world now stands, some such day of humiliation for England is at least possible. The suggested condition precedent of invasion, the destruction of the fleet by torpedoes attached by a new invention to our ships, has attracted many minds; and with the destruction of the regulars, the helplessness of the brave but half organized Volunteers, and the absence of arrangement, make up a picture which, fanciful as it is, we seem, as we read it, almost to have seen. It describes so exactly what we all feel that, under the circumstances, Englishmen, if refused time to organize, would probably do."—*Spectator (London.)*

"The extraordinary force and naturalness of the picture of the calamity itself, its consistency throughout, from the bits of the last *Times* leader, read by the unhappy volunteer in the City, to the description of the conduct of the Germans in the fatal Battle of Dorking, and in the occupation of the English homes which follows, seem to us as natural in its touches as can well be conceived."—*Pall Mall Gazette.*

"The Britons are stirred up by it as they have been by no one magazine article of this generation. The 'Fight at Dame Europa's School' did not hit the bull's eye of English feeling more squarely than this clever shot from old Maga. . . . . The verisimilitude is wonderful. We have read nothing like it outside of Robinson Crusoe."—*Journal of Commerce (New York.)*

THE SECOND ARMADA. A Chapter of Future History. Being a Reply to the Above. 12mo, paper covers. 10 cents.

The story of the German Conquest has produced a sensation both in America and England, having run into eight editions in this country in less than one month. The "London Times" of June 22d contained their version of the famous battle, with a totally different result however, and also had a long editorial on the two versions. This is given also with the reply.

"An intensely interesting little book, and must be read to be appreciated."—*Providence Gazette.*

OLIVER BUNCE.

ROMANCE OF THE REVOLUTION. Being true Stories of the Thrilling Adventures, Romantic Incidents, Hair-breadth Escapes and Heroic Exploits of the Days of '76. Laid paper, with six illustrations. 16mo, cloth, extra, $1.50.

While the principal events of the history of our glorious Revolution are known to every intelligent American, much remains to be disclosed of the inner history of the war, and the motives and patriotism of the people. There were deeds of individual daring, heroism worthy of the proudest days of Greece and Rome, dashing and hazardous enterprises, and hardships bravely borne, performed by subalterns and private soldiers in the grand army of heroes, which should never be forgotten. To collect and preserve the sketches of these almost forgotten passages of the war, as they originally appeared in the newspapers and private letters of that stirring period, and the stories told by scarred veterans round the blazing hearth-stone; these legends of the past; has been the object of this work, and the publishers are confident that none will rise from its perusal without acknowledging that "Truth is stranger than fiction," and with a deeper feeling of reverence for the heroes of the days of '76

"A collection of anecdotes and traditions relating to the War of Independence, which presents in a brilliant light chivalrous adventures called forth by the struggles of the early patriots for the freedom of their country. If some of the incidents here recorded have rather an apocryphal air, they yet serve to illustrate the spirit of the time, and present the truth more vividly to the imagination than the more formal pages of history. The volume is eminently adapted to popular reading."—*Harper's Magazine.*

CECIL B. HARTLEY.

LIFE OF THE EMPRESS JOSEPHINE, Wife of Napoleon I. With a fine Portrait on Steel. 16mo. Printed on fine laid paper. Cloth, extra, $1.50.

"Her career and her character were alike remarkable; surrounded by the demoralizations of the French Court, she was a Roman matron in stern rectitude, with a pre-eminent fidelity to a sensitive conscience; and blended comprehensive genius with a warm heart and a noble personal presence. She was the peer of Napoleon, and in some respects his superior. Her executive force was less, but her foresight was greater. It is to her that the index finger of history points, as an example of female grandeur. Napoleon got a divorce from her because he wished his seed to inherit the French Crown. The son born of his Hapsburg marriage died crownless, while the grandson of Josephine now wears the purple of France—this is more than poetic justice. * * * In the book before us, the story of her life is told in a simple, classic style, and possesses a fascination rarely met with in biography."—*Chicago Evening Journal.*

MRS. ANNA JAMESON.

LIVES OF CELEBRATED FEMALE SOVEREIGNS AND ILLUSTRIOUS WOMEN. Edited by Mary E. Hewitt. With four portraits on steel. 16mo, beautifully printed on laid paper. Cloth, extra, $1.50.

The celebrated Mrs. Jameson, who wields a powerful, ready, and pleasant pen, has taken hold of some of the leading events in the brilliant lives of some of the most world-noted women, and depicted them in very attractive colors. It is a lovely book for young ladies, and will give them a taste for history.

W. S. GILBERT.

THE BAB BALLADS; or, Much Sound and Little Sense. With 113 illustrations by the author. Square 12mo., cloth, bev. gilt edges, $1.75.

These Ballads, first published in periodicals, rapidly achieved a whimsical popularity, which soon demanded their publication in a collected form. Much of this is due to the series of inexpressibly funny drawings by the author, who is happy in being artist enough to interpret his own humor in these admirable sketches; we pity the man who cannot appreciate and enjoy them. The Ballads will rank with the best of Thackeray, Bon Gaultier, or Ingoldsby. Let every one who in these dull times has the blues, procure a copy as the cheapest remedy. While it is a nearly perfect *fac simile* of the English copy, it is only half the price.

"Everybody likes, occasionally, a little sensible nonsense. 'Mother Goose' is enjoyed in childhood, and something similar, but more advanced, is needed to provoke a smile on a wearied face in later years. This volume of comic poems answers such a purpose; some of them have a sly moral, while others are simply amusing from their supreme absurdity. The mirth is aided by the author's original cuts, which are quite in keeping with the poetry."—*Advance*, Chicago, the Great Religious Weekly.

C. M. METZ.

DRAWING-BOOK OF THE HUMAN FIGURE. With many Examples from the best Studies of the Old Masters, beautifully engraved in the first style of the art. Folio, half morocco, antique, $7.50.

H. B. STAUNTON.

THE AMERICAN CHESS PLAYER'S HANDBOOK. Teaching the Rudiments of the Game, and giving an analysis of all the recognized openings, amplified by appropriate games actually played by Morphy, Horwitz, Anderssen, Staunton, Paulson, Montgomery, Meek, and others. From the work of Staunton. Illustrated. 16mo, cloth, extra, bev. bds. $1.25.

"Among the great wants of students of this noble game of chess has been a handbook which should occupy a middle ground between the large and expensive work of Staunton and the ten cent guides with which the country is flooded. This want is happily supplied by the present volume. It is an abridgment of Staunton's work, and contains full accounts and descriptions of the common openings and defences, besides a large number of illustrative games and several endings and problems. It is a book which will be decidedly useful to all beginners in the game, and interesting to those who are already proficient in it."—*Peoria Transcript.*

"Will prove an invaluable guide for the admirers of the great and strategic game of chess. It should be in the hands of every chess-player."—*Galesburg Republican.*

"It is the best manual for the beginner with which we are acquainted,—exceedingly clear and intelligible."—*New Orleans Picayune.*

SARAH E. SCOTT.

EVERY-DAY COOKERY, FOR EVERY FAMILY. Containing nearly 1000 Receipts adapted to moderate incomes, and comprising the best and most economical methods of roasting, boiling, broiling and stewing all kinds of meat, fish, poultry, game and vegetables; simple and inexpensive instructions for making pies, puddings, tarts, and all other pastry; how to pickle and preserve fruits and vegetables; suitable cookery for invalids and children; food in season, and how to choose it; the best ways to make domestic wines and syrups, and ample receipts for bread, cake, soups, gravies, sauces, desserts, jellies, brandied fruits, soaps, perfumes, &c., &c., and full directions for carving. Illustrated. 16mo., cloth. Price, $1,25.

OTTO MÜLLER.

CHARLOTTE ACKERMAN. A Theatrical Romance, founded upon interesting facts in the life of a young artist of the last century. Translated from the German, by Mrs. Chapman Coleman and her Daughters, the translators of the Mulbach Novels. Paper, $1.00; cloth, $1.50.

"The author of this romance has acquired a solid reputation in Germany, and it is evident, from this translation, that it is deserved."—*San Francisco Daily Record.*

T. S. ARTHUR.

IDLE HANDS, AND OTHER STORIES. A new volume by this popular author. With six exquisite full-page cuts, engraved by Lauderbach. Square 8vo. Cloth, full gilt, $2.00.

"The most popular of all our American writers on domestic subjects."—*Godey's Lady's Book.*

"In the princely mansions of the Atlantic merchants, and in the rude log cabins of the backwoodsmen, the name of Arthur is equally known and cherished as a friend of virtue."—*Graham's Magazine.*

"As a writer of short moral stories and sketches, Mr. Arthur has probably no superior in this country. There is no mistaking the lesson intended to be taught. Thousands of young readers will hail the advent of this book with genuine joy."—*Indianapolis Evening News.*

"The name of T. S. Arthur is so well known as a charming writer for juveniles as well as for adults, that to commend this selection of beautiful and instructive stories, so tastefully gotten up by the enterprising publishers, would be but to put pencil and paint to finished work."—*Central Baptist, St. Louis.*

"The paper and printing are superb, and the binding, which allows the margin to be wide, is in the best style of green and gold. It is a book for the holidays."—*Worcester (Mass.) Daily Spy.*

FRIENDLY HANDS AND KINDLY WORDS. Stories illustrative of the Law of Kindness, the Power of Perseverance, and the Advantages of Little Helps. Eight fine illustrations by H. K. Browne, John Absolom, and the brothers Dalziel. 16mo, cloth, extra, 75 cents.

SMALL BEGINNINGS; OR, THE WAY TO GET ON. Beautifully illustrated with eight fine drawings by H. K. Browne, John Absolom and the brothers Dalziel. 16mo, cloth, extra, 75 cents.

THE ART OF DOING OUR BEST: As seen in the Lives and Stories ofs ome thorough Workers. Eight fine illustrations by H. K. Browne, John Absolom, and the brothers Dalziel. 16mo, cloth, extra, 75 cents.

YE BOOK OF SENSE. A new comic book. A Companion to Lear's celebrated Book of Nonsense. With thirty-two illustrations, brightly colored, Oblong 8vo, boards, $1.00; cloth, extra gilt, $1.50.

MISS H. B. McKEEVER,

Author of "The Flounced Robe, and What it Cost," Edith's Ministry," Woodcliffe," "Silver Threads," &c., &c.

These stories have the merit of being entertaining, instructive, and really much superior to the common run of Juveniles. The Springfield *Republican*, which is competent authority, pronounces them the best and handsomest Juvenile Books of the season."—*Lyons Republican.*

"Miss McKeever always writes with point and meaning, and in a manner to gain and hold the attention."—*Sunday-School Times.*

ELEANOR'S THREE BIRTHDAYS. "Charity seeketh not her own." Illustrated. 16mo., 295 pp., $1.00.

MARY LESLIE'S TRIALS. "Is not easily provoked." Illustrated. 16mo., $1.00.

LUCY FORRESTER'S TRIUMPHS. "Thinketh no evil, believeth all things, hopeth all things." Illustrated. 16mo. Price, $1.00.

R. M. BALLANTYNE.

New and beautiful editions of these world-renowned books, second only to those of Cooper and Marryatt, and better than those of Mayne Reid, in the pictures presented to the reader of wild life among the Indians, the hairbreadth escapes and fierce delights of a hunters' life, and the perils of "Life on the Ocean Wave." Ballantyne's name is well known to every intelligent boy of spirit. Leading the reader into the jungles and forests of Africa, sweeping over the vast expanse of our western prairies, "fast in the ice" of the Polar regions, or coasting the shores of sunny climes, he ever presents new and enchanting pictures of adventure or beauty to enchain the attention, absorb the interest, excite the feelings, and always at the same time instructing the reader.

THE GORILLA HUNTERS. A Tale of the Wilds of Africa. 16mo, illustrated, cloth, extra, $1.25.

"Thoroughly at home on subjects of adventure. Like all his stories for boys, thrilling in interest and abounding in incidents of every kind."—*The Quiver, London.*

THE DOG CRUSOE. A Tale of the Western Prairies. 16mo, illustrated, cloth, extra, $1.25.

"This is another of Mr. Ballantyne's excellent stories for the young. They are all well written, full of romantic incidents, and are of no doubtful moral tendency; on the contrary, they are invariably found to embody sentiments of true piety, manliness and virtue."—*Inverness Advertiser.*

GASCOYNE, THE SANDAL-WOOD TRADER. A Tale of the Pacific. 16mo, illustrated, cloth, extra, $1.25.

"'Gascoyne' will rivet the attention of every one, whether old or young, who pursues it."—*Edinburgh Courant.*

FREAKS ON THE FELLS; or, Three Months' Rustication. And why I did not become a Sailor. Illustrated, 16mo, cloth, extra, $1.25.

"Mr. Ballantyne's name on the title-page of a book, has for some years been a guaranty to buyers that the volume is cheap at its price."—*London Athenæum.*

THE WILD MAN OF THE WEST. A Tale of the Rocky Mountains. 16mo. Illustrated, cloth, extra, $1.25.

This is generally considered the best of Mr. Ballantyne's famous narratives of Indian warfare and border life. In this field he is second only to Cooper.

SHIFTING WINDS. A Story of the Sea. Cloth, extra, illustrated. $1.25.

R. M. BALLANTYNE—Second Series.

"Indulgent fathers and good uncles will look a long time before they will find books more interesting or instructive for boys than these. In the four volumes the author introduces his young readers to the wonders of the Arctic regions, the wild hunting-grounds of the Hudson's Bay Company, the rugged coast and midnight sun of Norway, and the exciting chase of the monsters of the deep on the pathless fields of the ocean. He is quite at home among the scenes he describes, and has the faculty of taking the boys along with him in his narrative, and making them feel at home in his company. His object is to give information and to inculcate sound principles of virtue, and he mingles enough of fancy with the fact and the moral lesson to make both more impressive and the more sure to be remembered. The boy who reads these volumes at the time when his mind is most susceptible to the stirring scenes of peril and adventure, will cultivate a taste for more complete and elaborate works of travel and discovery, in mature years."—*Rev. Daniel March, D.D.*

FIGHTING THE WHALES; or, Doings and Dangers on a Fishing Cruise. With four full-page Illustrations. 18mo., Illustrated, 75 cents.

AWAY IN THE WILDERNESS; or, Life Among the Red Indians and Fur-Traders of North America. 18mo., Illustrated, Cloth, extra, 75 cents.

It is one of the most delightful books this famed author has written. Whilst describing the exciting adventures of Indian life, he conveys new and attractive information about the far north portion of our continent.

Seldom, if ever, has there been a better description of life in the lands of the Hudson's Bay Company, than is found in this little work.

FAST IN THE ICE; or, Adventures in the Polar Regions. 18mo. Illustrated. Cloth, extra, 75 cents.

"Is attractive and useful. There is no more practical way of communicating elementary information than that which has been adopted in this series. When we see contained in 114 small pages, as in "Fast in the Ice," such information as men of fair education should possess about icebergs, Northern lights, Esquimaux, musk-oxen, bears, walruses, etc., together with all the ordinary incidents of an Arctic voyage, woven into a clear connected narrative, we must admit that a good work has been done, and that the author deserves the gratitude of young people of all classes."—*London Athenæum.*

CHASING THE SUN; or, Rambles in Norway. 18mo. Illustrated. Cloth, extra, 75 cents.

Describing a country almost new to us, the author tells of many strange natural curiosities, of the manners and customs of the people, and the curious modes of travel and conveyance.

ANNE BOWMAN.

THE BEAR HUNTERS OF THE ROCKY MOUNTAINS. 16mo. Illustrated. Cloth, extra, $1.25.

A story of trapper life in the Rocky Mountains. A better insight of real life in these uncivilized wilds is gained from books like this than from scores of the dry details of travellers.

ADVENTURES IN CANADA; or, Life in the Woods. 16mo. Illustrated. Cloth, $1.25.

This is not a mere work of fiction, but the true narrative of a bright boy who roughed it in the bush when Canada, the home of adventure and sporting, was much wilder than it is now. The boys, especially, will be charmed with the adventures with Indians, bears, and wolves, the racoon hunts and duck shooting; while the older class of readers will be drawn to it by its charming description of the scenery, and condition of what may, before long, become a part of the United States.

FOSTER'S TRANSLATION.

THE THOUSAND AND ONE NIGHTS; or, The Arabian Nights' Entertainment. A new edition. With eight full-page illustrations. Large 12mo, cloth, extra, $1.50.

"More widely diffused among the nations of the earth than any other product of the human mind. While it is read or recited to crowds of eager listeners in the Arab coffee-houses of Asia and Africa, it is just as eagerly perused on the banks of the Tagus, the Tiber, the Seine, the Thames, the Hudson, the Mississippi, and the Ganges. . . . While there are children on earth to love, so long will the 'Arabian Nights' be loved."—*Appleton's American Encyclopedia, article "Arabian Nights."*

D. W. BELISLE.

THE AMERICAN FAMILY ROBINSON; or, The Adventures of a Family lost in the Great Desert of the West. 16mo. Illustrated. Cloth, extra, $1.25.

DANIEL DE FOE.

THE LIFE AND ADVENTURES OF ROBINSON CRUSOE. Including a Memoir of the Author, and an Essay on his Writings. Large 12mo. Illustrated. Cloth, extra. Price, $1.50.

Carefully printed from new stereotype plates, with large, clear, open type, this is the best, as well as the cheapest, edition of this charming work published.

"Perhaps there exists no work, either of instruction or entertainment, in the English language, which has been more generally read and more universally admired, than 'The Life and Adventures of Robinson Crusoe.' It is difficult to say in what the charm consists, by which persons of all classes and denominations are thus fascinated; yet the majority of readers will recollect it as among the first works that awakened and interested their youthful attention, and feel, even in advanced life and in the maturity of their understanding, that there are still associated with Robinson Crusoe the sentiments peculiar to that period, when all is bright, which the experience of after-life tends only to darken and destroy."—*Sir Walter Scott.*

JEAN RODOLPHE WYSS.

THE SWISS FAMILY ROBINSON; or, The Adventures of a Father, Mother, and four Sons, on a Desert Island. Two parts, complete in one volume. illustrated. Large 12mo. Cloth, extra, Price, $1.50.

GRIMM.

POPULAR GERMAN TALES AND HOUSEHOLD STORIES. Collected by the Brothers Grimm. With nearly 200 illustrations by Edward H. Wehnert. Complete in one volume. New edition. Fine English cloth, bev. bds., full gilt back and side stamp, $2.50; half calf, gilt, $4.50.

The stories in these volumes are world-renowned, and they will continue to be read, as they long have been, in different languages, and to charm and delight not only the young, but many readers in mature life who love the recollections of childhood and its innocent diversions.

COUNTESS DE SEGUR.

FRENCH FAIRY TALES. Translated by Mrs. Coleman and her daughters. With ten full-page illustrations, by Gustave Dore and Jules Didier. 16mo, price, $1.50.

The Countess de Segur, the authoress of this charming work, and the mother of the wife of the French ambassador at Florence, the brilliant Baroness Malaret, is a Russian lady, and a daughter of the heroic Prince Rostopchin, who ordered the burning of Moscow, when Napoleon captured that devoted city.

"Not many of the fairy stories written for children are so admirably contrived or so charmingly written as these."—*Worcester Daily Spy.*

HARRY CASTLEMON.

THE SPORTMAN'S CLUB IN THE SADDLE. This is the first of the new Series of Six. The new volumes of this series will follow from time to time as rapidly as possible. Illustrated, 16mo, cloth, extra, black and gold, $1.25.

"The 'Sportsman's Club in the Saddle' is a splendid book for boys."—*Daily Journal, Newburgh, N. Y.*

"This story, we are quite certain, will please the boys immensely; it is full of amusing and exciting incidents."—*Worcester Daily Spy.*

"This is the first of the 'Sportman's Club Series' by one of the most popular authors of Juvenile books. The boys who love dogs and guns will enjoy this volume."—*Democrat, St. Louis.*

"A delightful writer is Castlemon. Has seen everything and remembers what he has seen. Describes scenes with great spirit, while all his volumes are full of incident and excitement. The author has a nice sense of the wants of boyhood, and produces such stories as give entire satisfaction to the future rulers of the republic."—*Albany Evening Post.*

"Mr. Castlemon is the author of several series of fascinating books for boys, and the present volume but adds to its reputation."—*Morning Herald, Utica. N. Y.*

"A spirited and lively sketch of the huntsman's sports. It is replete with exciting adventure wrought into the form of an animated story, and the young will follow its entertaining pages with unflagging interest."—*Albany Evening Journal.*

THE GUNBOAT SERIES. 6 vols., 16mo, illustrated. Cloth, black and gold, $7.50.

Frank the Young Naturalist. Frank on a Gunboat.
Frank in the Woods. Frank before Vicksburg.
Frank on the Lower Mississippi. Frank on the Prairie.

THE ROCKY MOUNTAIN SERIES. 3 vols., 16mo, illustrated. Cloth, black and gold, $3.75.

Frank among the Rancheros. Frank at Don Carlos' Rancho.
Frank in the Mountains.

THE GO-AHEAD SERIES. 3 vols., 16mo, illustrated. Cloth, black and gold, $4.50.

Go Ahead; or, The Fisher Boy's Motto.
No Moss; or, The Career of a Rolling Stone.
Tom Newcombe

JULIA McNAIR WRIGHT.

A MILLION TOO MUCH. A Temperance Tale. By Mrs. Julia McNair Wright, author of "Priest and Nun," "Almost a Nun," "New York Ned," "John and Demijohn," &c. 12mo. Fine cloth, $1.50.

"It is a valuable acquisition to the temperance literature of the day, probably the best work of the kind ever published, as it deals with absolute facts. It is really a wonderful book, and those who would work effectively in staying the tide of intemperance, would do well to circulate it."—*Bloomington Daily Leader.*

"It is infinitely better than stories of the kind generally are."—*Philadelphia Inquirer.*

"This story is one of the best pieces of temperance advocacy we have seen. Its scenes are graphic; its progress only too natural, and its conclusion a powerful warning. It is less of a tract than many of the same kind of tales, and merits attention for the freshness and force of its delineations."—*The Age, Philadelphia.*

"A first class temperance story. The career of one born with appetite for drink and with the means to gratify every wish is depicted with vigorous and rapid strokes in a well told story. * * We recommend this book for Sunday-school libraries."—"*The Pacific*," *San Francisco.*

MARGARET HOSMER.

Author of "Cherry, the Missionary," "Grandma Merritt's Stories," "The Voyage of the White Falcon," &c., &c.

LITTLE ROSIE'S FIRST PLAY DAYS. Illustrated. 18mo., 160 pp., 75 cents.

LITTLE ROSIE'S CHRISTMAS TIMES. Illustrated. 18mo., 160 pp., 75 cents.

LITTLE ROSIE IN THE COUNTRY. Illustrated. 18mo., 160 pp. 75 cents.

"Very nice children's books, indeed, and we only wish that we had more space to say so, and more time to say it in. Any present-giving fathers, mothers, uncles, aunts, brothers, or sisters, who have a care for the little people, may safely order these for home consumption."—*The Hartford Churchman.*

"A charming series of stories for the younger class of readers, full of interesting incidents and good moral and religious instruction, brought down to the comprehension of a child in such a way as to produce a salutary impression. They are calculated also to teach parents how to keep children employed in what is pleasant and useful, thus superseding the necessity of imposing so many restraints to keep them from evil. This is apt to be the great fault in the management of children. They are given nothing innocent and useful with which to employ their active, restless minds, and then parents wonder that they need be always in mischief. Rosie's mother better comprehended the wants of a child, and forestalled temptations to end by incentives to good."—*Springfield Daily Union.*

UNDER THE HOLLY; or, Christmas at Hopeton Grange. A Book for Girls. By MRS. HOSMER and MISS ——. 12mo. Illustrated. Cloth, extra, $1.50.

"And this we can and do most confidently recommend to parents who are faithfully striving to provide only wholesome food for the intellectual appetite of their children. The tone of the book is pure and healthful, the style easy and graceful, and the incidents are such as to give pleasure without at all kindling the passion for exciting fiction, which is so rampant among the young people of our day."—*Maryland Church Record.*

"This is entitled, 'A Book for Girls,' but it would interest the youth of either sex. It is a succession of tales told at the Christmas season. We can recommend them all for their interest and moral. It is for 'children of a larger growth,' not a mere story-book for the little ones."—*Philadelphia Daily Age.*

LENNY, THE ORPHAN; or, Trials and Triumphs. Illustrated, by Faber. 16mo. Price, $1.25.

"A story book of an orphan boy, who is thrown loose upon the world by a conflagration, in which his mother and only surviving parent is burnt. The varieties of experience, both sorrowful and happy, through which the boy passes, are wrought up into a story of no little power, and yet are such as often occur in actual life. The religious teachings of the book are good, and penetrate the entire structure of the story. We recommend it cordially to a place in the Sunday-school library."—*Sunday-School Times*, Philadelphia.

"The author of this book has written some of the best Sunday-school books which have recently been issued from the press of the American Sunday School Union. The volume before us portrays the trials of a little boy, who loses his mother in early life, and is subjected to the intrigues of a designing person, from which he obtains a happy deliverance. The story is well planned and written, and its moral and religious lessons are good."—*Weekly Freedman*, New Brunswick, N. J.

BARONESS MARTINEAU DES CHESNEZ.

LADY GREEN SATIN, AND HER MAID ROSETTE. Translated from the French. Illustrated. 1 vol., 12mo. Cloth, black and gold, $1.50.

This will be one of the most charming juveniles published this fall, both inside and outside.

HECTOR MALOT.

ROMAIN KALBRIS: HIS ADVENTURES ON SEA AND SHORE. Translated from the French by Mrs. JULIA MCNAIR WRIGHT, authoress of "Priest and Nun," "A Million Too Much," etc. Illustrated with 47 original French designs, by Emile Bayard, engraved in the handsomest style. 1 vol., 12mo. Cloth, black and gold, $2.50.

This will be the handsomest juvenile of the season, and is confidently recommended to the trade.

CAROLINE H. B. LAING.

THE SEVEN KINGS OF THE SEVEN HILLS. A Popular Ancient History of Rome, designed for Children. 16mo, illustrated, $1.

"A very attractive and well-told rendering of the fables of early Roman history. Everybody needs to know these stories, and this book will serve a good end in introducing them to children."—*The Nation, New York.*

"The early history of Rome is treated by the accomplished authoress of this work in a manner adapted to the comprehension and tastes of juvenile readers, without attempting to draw too sharp a line between the results of critical research and legendary fictions. Her little volume is highly entertaining, the language is chaste and graphic, and the narrative abounds with striking incidents."—*New York Tribune.*

THE HEROES OF THE SEVEN HILLS. A sequel to "The Seven Kings of the Seven Hills." A Child's History of Ancient Rome. 1 vol., 16mo. Illustrated. Cloth, black and gold, $1.

This little book, and the one to which it is a sequel, supply a want which has long been felt. The reception accorded the first one guarantees popularity to the coming volume.

MRS. S. C. HALLOWELL.

BEC'S BEDTIME, and other Stories from *The Christian Union.* 1 vol., 12mo. Illustrated. Cloth, black and gold, $1.50.

Mrs. Hallowell is well known as one of the most popular contributors to *The Christian Union*, and as a writer for children has a high standing.

VICTOR HUGO.

GAVROCHE, THE GAMIN OF PARIS. From "Les Miserables," by Victor Hugo. Translated and adapted by M. C. PYLE. A charming story. 16mo, cloth, black and gilt, $1.

"This story is a charming episode in Victor Hugo's famous book, 'Les Miserables.' It is a very touching and strongly drawn picture of Parisian life. The hero is a 'Gamin,' or street boy of Paris, who lives a vagabond life, and takes a precocious part in events of the great capital."—*The Age*, Philadelphia.

PAUL KONEWKA.

THE CATASTROPHE OF THE HALL. Illustrated with original drawings in Silhouette by the late Paul Konewka, in his most characteristic manner. Beautifully printed on tinted paper. Quarto. Boards, $1.00;

"A rhymed tale about three kittens, Beauty, Monkey and Dot, illustrated with silhouettes, by the late Paul Konewka, so spirited and so funny, that the children who read will be apt to agree with the boy on the title-page in being 'particularly glad that God *did* cats.'"—*New York Daily Tribune.*

MISCELLANEOUS.

THE LIBRARY; or, What Books to Read, and How to Buy them. A few practical hints, by an old Bookbuyer. 16mo, paper cover, 10 cents per copy; $8.00 per hundred.

Everybody has felt the want of a reliable guide in selecting books for their library. In this little manual, the author has endeavored first, in a preliminary essay, to point out how to read books to the best advantage, and how to buy them; second, what books to buy, by giving lists of some fifteen hundred volumes of standard works, such as are *necessary* to every well-selected library; these are given with the number of volumes, the best and different editions, and the prices. It thus forms a complete and intelligent guide, as to what is best to buy first, such as every person of any pretensions to literary taste should possess.

THOUGHTS OF PEACE; or, Strong Hope and Consolation for the Bearer of the Cross. From the last London edition. Beautifully printed on tinted paper, with carmine border. Square 16mo. Fine English cloth, bevelled boards, red edges, $1.50.

"Remarkable as the assertion is, that very many of the best works are the product of the chastened and afflicted in society, it is nevertheless true that the world is greatly enriched by the presence of invalid gifted minds in all ages. This delightful little volume is the product of one who has felt the acuteness of disease, and it illustrates the experience of one who has long been an invalid. The Scriptural texts, and poetic suggestions, evince a rich acquaintance with the scriptures and the poets. The book is beautifully printed on tinted paper, red line border, and richly bound. Many would prize it as a gift book."—*Pittsburg Gazette.*

"This is a reprint from the latest London edition, and is a beautiful little work, both in style of typography and binding, and in the sentiments judiciously selected and collated from the Sacred Scriptures and poets. It comprises three hundred and sixty-five of the most soul-comforting and inspiring texts of the Bible—one for each day of the year. Following each text is a short selection from some hymn, or sacred poem of corresponding sentiment. No better souvenir could be given to one having experienced some of life's sorrows—and who has not!—and who has learned to look for consolation to Holy Writ."—*Mauch Chunk Gazette.*

PAPA'S BOOK OF ANIMALS. Wild and Tame. Chiefly from the writings of Rev. J. G. WOOD and THOS. BINGLEY. With sixteen large and spirited drawings, by H. C. Bispham. Small 4to., fine English cloth, gilt, bev. bds. Price, $1.25.

SLOVENLY PETER; or, Cheerful Stories and Funny Pictures for Good Little Folks. With nearly two hundred engravings. Beautifully colored. Printed on heavy paper. Large 4to. Cloth, bevelled boards, extra, $1.75.

A new edition of this charming book, a standard among juveniles. Surely lessons of stern morality and humanity were never more pleasantly and effectually taught than in this book.

NORTHERN LIGHTS. Tales from Swedish and Finnish authors. Collected and translated by SELMA BORG and MARIE A. BROWN, the translators of the Schwartz Novels. 1 vol., 12mo. Illustrated. Cloth, black and gold, $1.50.

This collection of Northern Tales is full of beauty, and for imagination and poetic expression excels the far-famed tales of Hans Christian Andersen.

STANDARD FAIRY TALES. Containing Aladdin, Cinderella, Beauty and the Beast, Jack the Giant Killer, Red Riding Hood, Tom Thumb, Puss in Boots, and numerous other Favorites of the Nursery. Beautifully illustrated with eight full page engravings after designs by GUSTAV DORÉ and GEORGE CRUIKSHANK. 12mo, cloth, extra, black and gold, $1.50.

ADVENTURES BY LAND AND SEA. Perils, Hardships, and Escapes; taken from the most famous travels. 1 vol. Small 4to. Profusely illustrated. Cloth, black and gold, and illuminated side. $2.

PERILOUS INCIDENTS IN THE LIVES OF SAILORS AND TRAVELLERS. Small 4to. Profusely illustrated. Cloth, black and gold, and illuminated side. $2.

These are companion volumes, and will be great favorites for the holiday season.

M. C. PYLE.

MINNA IN WONDERLAND, AND ROLAND AND HIS FRIENDS. A charming new juvenile. Beautifully illustrated. Cloth, black and gold, 75 cents.

ROSE VALLEY LIBRARY. 6 vols. 32mo. Illustrated. In neat box. Per vol., 25 cents.

Robinson Crusoe.	Discontented Tom.
Eva Bruen.	Edith Locke.
Willie and Ned.	Ben Benson.

ALADDIN; or, The Wonderful Lamp. With fifteen large and beautiful illustrations, by F. O. C. Darley. Small 4to, fine English cloth, gilt, bev. bds., $1.50.

THE HAPPY CHILD'S PICTURES OF ANIMALS AND BIRDS. 4to. Illustrated with large colored pictures from drawings of animals and birds, by Harrison Wier. Fancy boards. Price 45 cents.

MOTHER GOOSE'S COMPLETE EDITION OF HER RHYMES, CHIMES, AND MELODIES. 128 pp., profusely illustrated, colored, square 12mo. Fancy boards, 60 cents; cloth, gilt, 75 cts.

LETTER WRITERS.

THE GENTLEMAN'S LETTER-WRITER. Bound in boards, cloth back. 139 pp. Price, 35 cents.

THE LADY'S LETTER-WRITER. Bound in boards, cloth back. 139 pp. Price, 35 cents,

THE COMPLETE LETTER-WRITER. For the use of Ladies and Gentlemen; containing both the above bound in one volume. 273 pp. Cloth, gilt. Price, 75 cents.

www.ingramcontent.com/pod-product-compliance
Lightning Source LLC
LaVergne TN
LVHW010239110826
845151LV00004B/1336

* 9 7 8 1 4 2 5 5 2 3 7 4 9 *